THE CREATION OF CHAOS

SUNY Series in Rhetoric and Theology

David Tracy and Stephen H. Webb, Editors

THE CREATION OF CHAOS

*William James and the Stylistic Making
of a Disorderly World*

Frederick J. Ruf

State University of New York Press

Published by
State University of New York Press, Albany

For information, address the State University of New York Press,
State University Plaza, Albany, NY 12246

Production by Christine M. Lynch
Marketing by Theresa A. Swierzowski

Library of Congress Cataloging-in-Publication Data

Ruf, Frederick J., 1950-
     The creation of chaos : William James and the stylistic making of
a disorderly / Frederick J. Ruf.
          p.   cm.
     Includes bibliographical references and index.
     ISBN 0-7914-0701-2 (alk. paper). — ISBN 0-7914-0702-0 (pbk. :
alk. paper)
     1. James, William, 1842-1910—Literary art. I. Title.
 B945.J24R84   1991
 191—dc20   90-44858
                                                                CIP

10 9 8 7 6 5 4 3 2 1

To Christine, Joanna, and Jesse:
with whom life's always joyful chaos

And to Frederick M. J. Ruf (1917-1988)
who probably saw classicism here, not chaos

Contents

Abbreviations

EP	James, William. *Essays in Philosophy. The Works of William James.* Ed. Frederick H. Burkhardt, Fredson Bowers, and Ignas K. Skrupskelis. Cambridge: Harvard University Press, 1978.
ERE	———. *Essays in Radical Empiricism. Works.* 1976.
ERM	———. *Essays in Religion and Morality. Works.* 1982.
LWJ	———. *The Letters of William James.* 2 vols. Ed. Henry James, Jr. New York: Longman, 1920.
PU	———. *A Pluralistic Universe. Works.* 1977.
Prag.	———. *Pragmatism: A New Name for Some Old Ways of Thinking. Works.* 1975.
PP	———. *The Principles of Psychology.* 3 vols. *Works.* 1981.
Talks	———. *Talks to Teachers on Psychology and to Students on Some of Life's Ideals. Works.* 1983.
VRE	———. *The Varieties of Religious Experience. Works.* 1985.
WB	———. *The Will to Believe and Other*

Essays in Popular Philosophy.
Works. 1979.

Perry   Ralph Barton Perry. *The Thought and*
Character of William James. 2
vols. Boston: Little, Brown and
Company; 1935.

Acknowledgments

This book came into being because of the inspiration of three men: Gordon D. Kaufman, whose directness and intelligence made me think more strongly and defend myself more skillfully than ever before; James Engell, whose great learning, standards of clarity, and knowledge of literary matters greatly improved the chapters on style, helped engender any stylistic grace that the book itself might have, and sharpened my awareness of many of the book's issues; and Richard R. Niebuhr who first engaged my interest in William James, and whose deep understanding of James provided me with a constant test of the adequacy of my ideas.

I would also like to thank William A. Graham for his early encouragement when this was only a very dim idea, and my friends and colleagues: Alan Hodder, Steve Compagna-Pinto, Davis Ayres, Carol Zaleski, and Win Quayle for their frequent stimulation. Harvey Oxenhorn enriched both it and me, and I only wish he had lived to see it in print. Colleagues in the Theology Department and students in my classes at Georgetown University have also been a source of great inspiration. Finally, I would like to acknowledge the wonderful support and enrichment of my family: Christine Ruf, and Nelle and Frederick Ruf. I hope this book serves as adequate homage to all of them.

Introduction

William James, stylist

"Style is not my forte," declared William James very early in his writing career.[1] It is a disarming and misleading comment coming from a man who would become not only one of America's most original thinkers, but one of its most original philosophical stylists, as well. Nearly everyone who writes about James feels compelled to comment on his manner of writing. To Leon Edel, the biographer of Henry James, William is "a writer of vivid and lucid scientific papers, of works in psychology and philosophy, in a vigorous, muscular style that abounded in image and example and created an effect of rich spontaneous talk."[2] The psychologist Stanley Hall praised the author of The *Principles of Psychology* as "an impressionist in psychology."[3] William Dean Howells said of the same work that "nothing could be more winning than the informality of his discourse; it captivates the average human being to find that the study of his mind is not necessarily allied to a frigid decorum."[4] In his study, Gerald E. Myers observes that James's personality "permeated his posture, gestures, clothing, voice—and especially his language," and points out James's strong use of humor and visual imagery.[5] There have also been more equivocal assessments. Charles Peirce spoke of James's manner as "slap-dash," and James's biographer, Ralph Barton Perry, characterized his style as "meanderings, zigzags, and circles."[6] In short, the manner in which James wrote has struck his readers as being as highly unconventional and original as his thought, though opinions vary as to whether that manner served his thought or detracted from it.

Yet although there has been a great deal written on James, including a number of notable works over the past several years, his style has been more the subject of remark than study.[7] James's pragmatism, his radical empiricism, his relationship to phenomenology, his place in the intellectual history of the nineteenth century, his contributions to the philosophy of religion: these and much else have been explored to our considerable benefit. James would, I'm certain, be greatly pleased that there can be such a wealth of interpretations of his writings and significance. Yet it seems an oversight to focus solely on what James had to say, and not to explore how he chose to say it. James is a figure whom we should study closely as a writer as well as a mind.

That is my topic in this book: what James's style accomplishes. Yet, paying close attention to the manner in which a philosopher writes may strike some as being out of balance. Style is usually merely the object of remark because we believe that what is of interest about an important thinker is the thought, not how that thought has been expressed. We want to arrive at the ideas, and we are grateful if the journey to them is not tedious or unduly delayed. If we are very lucky, we are entertained along the way with wit and vivid illustrations, but the purpose of style is just to get us to our destination. Or so we believe.

William James is a writer whose style does not efface itself, refusing to be a mere vehicle. In the first place, we are always aware that there is a man writing the words. James's books present aspects of his personality with which we easily become involved. Yet James's is not the only voice heard in his books: aside from generous quotations, he dramatizes, speaking in many voices. "Failure, then, failure! so the world stamps us at every turn," he says for the sick soul in *The Varieties of Religious Experience*; "Hollo! thinkumbob again!" says a polyp in *The Principles of Psychology*.[8] In addition to the multiplicity of voices, both books contain a grand eclectic mix of styles, even of genres. There are laments, satires, hymns, meditations, exhortations, narratives, and much else in the *Principles*, and a similar though diminished plurality of forms in the *Varieties*. James's works are not novels, nor would anyone consider them light reading, but a festival of variety goes on in their pages. The question is: Why?

My answer is chaos. It is not a facetious remark. If there are two of James's expressions that everyone knows, one is "stream of consciousness," and the other is "blooming, buzzing confusion." Both are, I will argue, chaotic. Both are characterized by fluidity, indeterminacy, and multiplicity. In fact, James uses those qualities, plus continuity, vagueness, change, chance, and any number of streams to challenge innumerable concepts that he feels are too rigid or too static. On one side we have the "block universe" with which James is so dissatisfied, and on the other the "Dyak's head," that mere collection of "innumerable feathers, leaves, strings, beads, and loose appendices of every description [that] float and dangle from [a dried human head]," an image that James seems to find endlessly fascinating.[9] Multiplicity, indeterminacy, vagueness, fluidity, chance, and change run through James's thoughts from early to late. How can we characterize them as a whole? I suggest *chaos* and will argue for the aptness of that collective term in my first three chapters. It is not because James uses the term himself, for he does so relatively rarely and in a highly restricted sense, but because as a whole these qualities function in a way that may best be described as chaotically.[10]

Which brings us back to the grand eclectic mix of James's style. It might seem natural at this point to claim that James's manner of writing is in some sense chaotic, too, but I do not wish to say that. Instead I would like to make the more controversial claim for style, one that may return it to the interest of theologians and philosophers. I believe that the manner in which a work is written has a truly profound effect on its readers. Far from being a mere vehicle for ideas, a work's form[11] plays a critical role in how we view the world. In Nelson Goodman's terms, it is an element in worldmaking: style *creates* our worlds. And the world that *The Principles of Psychology* and *The Varieties of Religious Experience* make is a chaotic world. That is, the styles of those books function to inculcate in readers the sense that the world is, in the precise sense I will develop, "chaotic."

If that is so, James's works participate in more than the development of modern psychological, philosophical, and

religious thought. They also stand in the history of the
chaotic, a religious orientation with roots that go back to Job
and beyond, and having one important branch in Pascal,
Kierkegaard, Nietzsche, and Karl Barth, and another in Blake,
Schleiermacher, and deconstructive theologians like Mark
Taylor. That, indeed, is a major motivation for this study, to
see just how it is that James proposes that his readers "front
life," to use one of his metaphors for the function of religion.
Paradoxically, chaotic views such as those stretching from
Job to Kierkegaard to James serve to orient readers in relation
to themselves, their surroundings, and their destination by
offering a useful sense of *disorientation*. The final chapter in
this study will attempt to place James's "chaotic" worldview
and his stylistic creation of it in a more general framework of
religious disorientation. In case there is any confusion, then,
this is an examination of William James as a *religious* thinker,
but one whose manner of writing plays a far more prominent
and constructive role than has generally been acknowledged.
Indeed, readers have often felt that they are moved more
than intellectually by James's books. That may be because
those works function religiously by providing a chaotic orientation.

   "Meandering, zigzags, and circles" was Perry's description
of James's style. To James Sully, that was lamentable for what
the *Principles* needed was a "rigorous sequence [and] progressive development.[12] What I would like to propose in this
book is that James's peculiar style perfectly suited his
thought, for he spoke of a chaotic self in a chaotic world, and
the manner in which he wrote shaped just such a world for
his readers. To Plato, Ovid, and other classical writers, chaos
was simply there, and a demiurge had to shape and order it
into a cosmos. My suggestion is that James did not start with
chaos but *created* it, and that remarkable end was accomplished largely through his "meanderings, zigzags, and circles."

1
The Maelstrom:
The Chaotic in The Principles of
Psychology: Part 1

Introduction

The Principles of Psychology is a monumental work, fourteen hundred pages in the original edition, twelve years in the making, encyclopedic in its scope. It is a work well worth comparing to *Moby Dick* or *War and Peace* as a masterpiece, as Jacques Barzun indeed does.[1] It is not just that it is a large volume or a classic, but that it is inexhaustible, a work not merely of learning but of wisdom from which we emerge not merely better informed but changed.

The *Principles* changes us because it captures and challenges us, embroiling us in difficulty, not allowing us to remain the same. That is not because the book is strident or contentious or polemical. It speaks, in fact, in the friendliest of manners. The voice that comes through these pages is very much like that of James himself. As Gay Wilson Allen says, "Few teachers [or men, we might add] have been so loved and valued as a friend."[2] Yet, the *Principles* is nonetheless a work that creates difficulty. How is this done? I think we can get an idea by looking at James's presentation of other works in psychology.

In his preface to the Italian edition of the *Principles*, James says that his text presents the state of contemporary knowledge in psychology, "the classic tradition, the associationist analysis, the psychogenetic speculations, the experimental methods, the biological conceptions, and the pathological extensions of the field."[3] All of it adds up to a state of "chaotic fermentation" in psychology, James notes. Chaotic fermentation: this is a provocative phrase. Matters are in disarray, but a disarray from which James does not wish to pro-

1

tect us. The expression indicates his ambivalence. Psychology may be in turmoil, and it may, therefore, have its "crudities," but it's a productive, not a threatening turmoil. He does not really want to eliminate the chaos, for that would mean losing the fermentation and the growth.

In fact, James not only omits none of the conflict in the field, he accentuates it. He allows the disputants to speak, quoting to a degree that disturbed Sully who felt a man so qualified to write his own book "would have done well not to let others contribute quite so much to his pages."[4] He reminds us of the acrimony between disputants through asides and emphasizes disagreements through the organization of his chapters. But the conflict in interpretations is important to this book, as is the presentation of so many voices speaking from his pages. James himself becomes yet another voice, sometimes seeking to settle disputes, sometimes letting them stand, and sometimes presenting his view as just another option. Of course, it is James's book; he's the one who tells the story of the conflicts and achievements in the study of the mind. Yet, to an unusually large degree he allows his readers to feel the strife and struggle. "Terrible recriminations have, as usual, ensued between the investigators," he notes in the chapter on "The Functions of the Brain."[5]

Moreover, James compels his readers to participate in the disputes concerning the nature of the mind. Barzun compares the *Principles* to *Moby Dick* because it is "the narrative of a search," a search for the human mind.[6] James involves his readers in that search through many techniques that this study will explore, but more generally through his use of the introspective method. In the preface to the Italian edition, he proposes to diminish the confusion of the "chaotic fermentation" of interpretations by "confining myself to what could be immediately verified by everyone's own consciousness. . . . [It is] the living reality with which I wish to bring my reader into direct concrete acquaintance."[7] Introspection may, as James claims, disallow many psychological theories, but it does not eliminate confusion. Not only do we reach few fixed answers through James's method, but the consideration of mental life is sufficient "to leave a chaotic impression on the observer."[8]

James wants his readers to feel the chaos of interpretations through reading his text; he wants them to experience a sort of chaos through examining their own minds. The chaotic is fertile, so if we want fermentation—growth, change, and improvement—then we must not only tolerate, but actively encourage the chaotic. It seems to me that the *Principles* is an important work because it embroils us in chaos, which can be a creative medium, as it was for Plato's demiurge.

In fact, chaos is not only something that James allows to remain, not just something he encourages. Rather, the chaotic is something that James creates. He has an enormous affinity for the chaotic; consequently he sees it wherever he looks when he turns his attention to the psychological. In all, James constructs a view of the mind where the chaotic is ubiquitous. Ultimately, the scope of James's view of the chaotic makes it a religious worldview, and the chaotic is able to perform the paradoxical function of orienting humans, a role I will discuss later in this book.

James and chaos: the critical view

I am not the first to see chaos in James. Many of his critics have been dismayed by it from the start. The year after James's death, his friend, colleague, and philosophical opponent Josiah Royce, spoke of James as one of three enduring American thinkers, but criticized his religious philosophy as "indeed chaotic." Royce felt that James's error lay in his individualism and reliance on the subconscious that left religion "in the comparatively trivial position of a play with whimsical powers." James's pragmatism, too, was denounced by Royce as anarchic for its neglect of a communal dimension. Lacking a social context, James's notion of experience was, in the Pauline metaphor, just a "tinkling cymbal."[9]

It is really no wonder that Royce saw chaos in James and considered that chaos a "profound and momentous error."[10] James issued a challenge to the thought of his time, and he did it not by offering an alternative but by attempting to dissolve presuppositions about such matters as the status of truth, the nature of experience, and the state of the mind. His pragmatism traded the stability of a correspondence notion of truth for the instability of creation and evaluation, a proposition that is still enormously disquieting today.[11] James's radical empiricism, in the words of William Dean, praised confusion, turning aside the Cartesian requirement of "clear and distinct" ideas for a more appropriate "aboriginal sensible muchness."[12] Finally, his notion of the stream of consciousness washed away the distinctness of sensation, reasoning, and willing into what seemed—and seems—to some like a very muddy flow indeed.

Louis J. Halle is an example of a thinker who condemns Jamesian positions for being chaotic. Halle's *Out of Chaos* chronicles the progressive creation of order out of chaos in the human and physical universes. "What is basic to being," he claims, "is the tendency of its elements to combine in forms or patterns that have coherence and symmetry, that have a larger order. This seems to be a single progressive tendency to bring order out of chaos." Halle's view of chaos is a traditional one; he sees it as confused and threatening, even unaesthetic. He contrasts it with a "perfect order" that is manifested in mental conceptions and physical being on the largest scale.[13]

Though Halle does not write of James directly, he isolates two particularly Jamesian notions for criticism. The first is indeterminacy. James is like Marlow in "Heart of Darkness": he loves the blank spaces on the map. It isn't especially that James is drawn to the unknown, not that he wants to explore it and make it known; rather, it is important to James that the universe be open, that there be possibility, chance, and pluralism. Indeterminacy is a central aspect of James's view of knowledge and morality because it leaves room for novelty and for action. "Indeterminism . . . gives us a pluralistic, restless universe, in which no single point of view can ever take in the whole scene."[14] James acknowledges that the embracing of chance will seem like chaos, and so it does to Halle who states that "because we cannot conceive of . . . an order except as one of strict cause and effect, in which every item is predetermined by antecedent causes that are predetermined, in turn, by their own antecedent causes, our logic requires us to equate indeterminism with chaos."[15]

Through the center of the largest blank space on Marlow's map flowed a mighty river, and so, too, is the stream of consciousness central to the mind and to the *Principles*. It is a metaphor that has left an indelible mark on twentieth-century culture. To Halle the stream of consciousness is but an example of incoherence and chaos. He focuses on its depiction in *Ulysses* where it is "like an alimentary canal, through which half-digested sensations and recollections follow one another in a more-or-less incoherent succession."[16] While Joyce might have enjoyed that characterization, especially as applied to Leopold Bloom, to Halle it is a condemnation. For Halle, the stream of consciousness reverses the progression toward order and allows chaos to break out.

It seems clear that if Halle turned his attention to James, it would be with disapproval. He would certainly be as disquieted as Royce or as Freud who also labeled pragmatism anarchic.[17] But there are also others who spy chaos in James's thought and are not bothered by it, seeing it instead as valuable. Charlene Haddock Seigfried analyzes several kinds of chaos operating in James.[18] One is the totality of sense impressions that are chaotically disordered. In contrast to that absolute chaos is a quasi-chaos in which the world has a multiplicity and abundance of relations from which we must select, but that is a chaos without such selection. Though she is not explicit about it, Seigfried also sees a chaotic aspect of consciousness since James's "knowledge of acquaintance" involves an awareness of this multiplicity of relations.[19] The stream of consciousness, then, with its wide-flowing "fringe" is as chaotic as is the external quasi-chaos. Finally, chaos is not only a description of the world or of consciousness but a principle explaining why the universe resists all attempts to unify it. "No relationship that unifies various experiences has been found which unifies all experience whatever. Other experiences are always left over which appear chaotic when judged by their coherence with the given relation."[20] In all,

Seigfried uses the term *chaos* to characterize James not as a sign of approbation but as the most appropriate designation, and one that indicates not the error and confusion in his thought but its power and novelty.

David M. LaGuardia also sees chaos in James. He feels it exists even more widely than Seigfried does, and he admires it more frankly. According to LaGuardia, the flux of the world is the primary chaos in James. As in Seigfried, this chaos is a source of wealth, not only because of the festival of reality that can invigorate our thoughts, but also because the awareness of constant mutation removes the tendency to become fixed in our formulations: "the death of fixity is the mother of ripeness," summarizes LaGuardia.[21]

In addition, chaos affects the notions of truth and freedom, and, accordingly, takes on a dual character. Novelty becomes a crucial aspect of truth since the flux of reality must be integrated with the ideas we already hold. Because the flux is always new, truth must be new, too.[22] Such a notion of truth is another instance of the value of chaos, of its ability to save us from the stale and rigid. But the flux of the world also offers a severe challenge since there is a great deal of insecurity without a unified design to the universe, and human responsibility in shaping its world is weighty. Humans are free to create their own worlds but also obliged to "decreate" outworn ones and are not allowed simply to let things be. While we can be burdened by the freedom in chaos, ultimately LaGuardia sees chaos in somewhat sacramental terms, for there is a "baptismal renewal" that results from "immersion into the dynamic flow."[23]

While he terms James a "Connoisseur of Chaos" like Wallace Stevens, and hence one aware of the vast significance of the flux about us, LaGuardia does not make the move from chaos to the chaotic. That is, like Seigfried, he places James in a worldly chaos that has vast significance for his thoughts, both pragmatism and radical empiricism rising from it, but he maintains a substantive notion of chaos: chaos is a sea about us. LaGuardia does not see that chaos is more useful as an adjective, as a description of James's thought itself. The flux of the world is just one instance of a notion that pervades

James. While it is enormously useful to see that the flux of the world is a chaos and that it has consequences for James's theories of truth and action, it is more useful to look at this basic quality of his thinking, his affinity for the chaotic.

In fact, the chaotic is a worldview in James's thoughts. I do not mean anything as formal as Stephen C. Pepper's "world hypotheses," which are of unlimited scope, which all facts will corroborate, and of which there are only four.[24] Nor am I speaking of the sort of worldview Ninian Smart makes such use of, since the motivational role of worldviews is of primary importance to him.[25] James's pragmatism or his radical empiricism might be worldviews of those sorts. Yet since the chaotic is so pervasive in James's thought, being not so much a topic or a theme as a chief term of his thought, it seems to have the scope of a worldview. There may be two ways to look at the matter. On the one hand, the chaotic seems to have a lot in common with Pepper's "root metaphors." According to Pepper, someone trying to understand the world seizes upon some commonsense fact and uses it as a basic analogy. Such an analogy eventually may generate a world hypothesis.[26] Like the root metaphor, the chaotic is an image and it has considerable fertility, being applicable in many areas, perhaps tending toward unlimited scope. On the other hand, it would be wrong to relegate the metaphorical to secondary status simply because it is not developed or refined. The worlds that Nelson Goodman writes of can be made by works of art, and those worlds need no philosophical elaboration to be viable worlds. For Goodman it is reference, expression, and exemplification that create worlds, and a notion like the chaotic would seem to do so as well as anything more explicitly theoretical.[27]

What I propose to do in the first three chapters of this book is to examine the chaotic view of the world as it lies implicit in *The Principles of Psychology* and *The Varieties of Religious Experience*. This is half of the work of the present study for it is only once we understand how it is that James imagines himself and the world that we can see that his style is an instrument in the creation of that world.[28] Chapters 4 and 5, then, will be detailed analyses of the role played by style in the creation of a chaotic self and world analogous to those discussed in the earlier chapters. Superficially this may seem to be two books, one on chaos and one on James's style. Yet in fact, the rhetorical readings of the later chapters absolutely depend upon what is developed earlier. All this, I must reiterate, is fueled by an interest in James's *religious* significance: it is a study of the stylistic creation of a chaotic world that functions religiously. The religious nature of James's chaotic world will, in turn, be more explicitly addressed in the final chapter.[29]

Yet a reader might have felt an uneasiness far before this point, for though I have cited a half dozen people describing the *chaos* in James's work, it is not at all clear what they mean when they use the word or even if they mean the same thing. In fact, a considerable degree of chaos seems to characterize the uses of *chaos*, so it seems best to begin to find some order.

The chaotic: "chaosmos"

The *Oxford English Dictionary* lists two primary meanings for *chaos*. The first is the "formless void . . . out of which the cosmos or order of the universe was evolved," a standard of cosmological speculation reaching back to Hesiod. The second definition is figurative, "a state resembling that of primitive chaos; utter confusion and disorder."[30] James's predominant use of *chaos* follows both senses. He speaks of consciousness creating something "whereof the potency was not given in the mere outward atoms of the original chaos."[31] He also extends such speculation from the cosmological to the epistemological, our different individual views of the world lying "embedded in the primordial chaos of sensations."[32] Equally common are figurative references to chaos as an absence of order, sense, or shape. He states that "only those items which I notice shape my mind—without selective interest, experience is an utter chaos . . . without it the consciousness of every creature would be a gray chaotic indiscriminateness, impossible for us even to conceive."[33]

Yet *chaos* is used in more varied ways than the *OED*

might lead us to believe. In general, *chaos* seems to be defined through what it is not. *Chaos* is the lack of order or structure or form. Cosmologically it is the absence of cosmos, as in Ovid's chaos, "a rude and indigested Mass."[34] Shakespeare brings that disorder down to earth in *Troilus and Cressida*: "When the planets / In evil mixture to disorder wander" the result is not only the plagues, storms, and earthquakes of nature but the mutiny, patricide, and rank injustice of society. This utter lack of "degree, priority and place, / Insisture,[35] course, proportion, season, form, / Office, and custom, in all line of order" he terms chaos.[36] Finally, Pascal sees an inner want of order.

> What a chimera then is man! What a novelty! What a monster, what a chaos, what a contradiction, what a prodigy! Judge of all things, imbecile worm of the earth; depository of truth, a sink of uncertainty and error; the pride and refuse of the universe![37]

What Pascal sees us lacking is the balance and proportion of reason and innate nature whereby we could truly understand ourselves. In great part, *chaos* is used by these writers to denote what does not exist, rather than what does. Their eyes are on the orderly progression of the cosmos or the hierarchical structure of nature and society or the harmony of reason and nature, and chaos signifies their absence.

Yet, *chaos* is not used wholly negatively, even in these examples. It is not just the lack of order these writers see; it is disorder. That is, when we read the passage from Ovid, Shakespeare, or Pascal, we do not only imagine the absence of "degree, priority, and place," we imagine something more tangible. We imagine *chaos*. The word connotes an undigested lump in Ovid, civil strife in Shakespeare, a confused mixture in Pascal. Some concrete image of chaos is unavoidable, and that image is more than an operational negation of form and order; the unformed has form; the disordered has order; the unstructured has structure. That is the paradoxical nature of the chaotic: it signifies the formless but it must do so through some form or other.[38] Joyce is right when he speaks of "chaosmos" in *Finnegans Wake*: every chaos is a cosmos.[39]

The argument for the figured nature of all experience, not to mention all language, reaches back at least to Kant's insistence on the active human involvement in all experience, to the extent that experience receives its shape from the shaping power of the knowing mind. It would be a contradiction for the mind to form experience formlessly.[40] Ernst Cassirer certainly contributes to such ideas by his emphasis on the importance of symbols that he takes to be "not the imitations but *organs* of reality." And those symbols, too, have definite form. "For the mind, only that can be visible which has some definite form; but every form of existence has its source in some particular way of seeing, some intellectual formulation and intuition of meaning."[41] Gordon D. Kaufman summarizes the importance of such thought for theology when he argues that the experience of transcendence, ultimacy, or the infinite would be impossible without the guidance of linguistic symbols. "These symbols are not bare and empty names for the experiences which they supposedly designate. They carry nuances of meaning derived from their various uses in the language and their connections with other terms."[42] In sum, a conception of chaos as absolutely without form would be impossible for us. Any conception of the formless would be of some form or other.

This paradox is managed in a variety of different ways. At its extreme is the desire to communicate *utter* disorder, such as we might see in Othello's anguish over Desdemona.

> Excellent wretch! Perdition catch my soul
> But I love thee! And when I love thee not,
> Chaos is come again.[43]

We might see an extreme, too, in Hobbes's condemnation of the commonwealth founded on some basis other than God's sovereignty as "by this means destroying all laws, both divine, and humane, reduce all Order, Government, and Society, to the first Chaos of Violence, and Civill warre."[44] Both men seem to want to push toward an unimaginable limit of disorder, and the strength of their depictions of emotional anguish or civil strife depends on how extreme the word *chaos* is.

On the other hand, we might not see the same sense of utter disorder in Kate Chopin's description of Edna Pontellier's awakening view of the world as "necessarily vague, tangled, chaotic, and exceedingly disturbing."[45] The late nineteenth-century novelist depicts confusion but not utter confusion, a tangle not an absolutely disordered knot. In speaking of the "old chaos of the sun," Wallace Stevens, too, is not aiming at quite the degree of disorder Shakespeare and Hobbes are. The spirits are dead in "Sunday Morning," so all we have is the "old chaos of the sun," but that chaos is full of deer and quail and wild berries and, significantly, the undulating *forms* of pigeons.[46] Notions of the chaotic can be less extreme, perhaps more mundane because all notions of chaos are inevitably figured. It seems difficult to maintain an austere notion of the chaotic; easy for the notion to move toward the common, as in Chopin and Stevens. The result is a loosening of the paradox. Some form must be used to express the unformed, but then chaos loses more and more of the power of its "utter confusion and disorder," until, in those like Chopin and Stevens, it is not "utter" and it is scarcely confusion or disorder.

Moreover, the threatening character of the chaotic in the extreme cases can become lost in the less extreme. Othello's emotional chaos drives him to Desdemona's death and his own. The chaos in Hobbes's *Leviathan* is a strong threat indeed. Yet Stevens's old chaos of the sun has a relaxed, native feel to it. It is the

old dependency of day and night,
Or island solitude, unsponsored, free[47]

Even more notable is Henry Adams's view that "chaos often breeds life, when order breeds habit."[48] In both cases, chaos still means a disorder, but in both it is an order that has become oppressive, and its absence means some sort of a liberation. Chaos is messy, confusing, even risky, but it is preferable to an order that is stifling or wrong.

As we saw, James's use of the word *chaos* adheres more closely to the disordered extreme than to the more moderate, but we need not leave the chaotic at that. The sort of suspicion of rigid structure or system that we see in Adams or of an alienating order in Stevens is not only congenial but essential to James. It lies behind his view of consciousness, the self, sensation, attention, reasoning, willing, and much else. It is he who criticizes the carving of our consciousness into mere reflections of things, with an identical rigid outline and division of parts.[49] It is James who takes particular aim at "old fogeyism" as the enslavement to "the stock conceptions with which we have once become familiar,"[50] or at the "block universe" that he opposes with the "wider sea of possibilities."[51] James's writing is replete with such statements. Thomas R. Martland sees James as primarily concerned with change and becoming as opposed to "structure in one form or other."[52] Barnard P. Brennan characterizes James as oriented toward flux, novelty, and chance and resistant to regular pattern, predictability, and completeness.[53] James does not counter rigid structure or system with an explicit chaos; rather, there is a variety of notions that James puts forth to challenge fixity: the vague, change, fluidity, chance, indeterminacy, continuity, multiplicity, and any number of streams—of consciousness, of selves, of neural action—as well as other bodies of water. All of these dissolve those aspects of the hard-edged and the rigid that James finds violate introspection, are untenable philosophically or scientifically, or result in undesirable consequences.

It is my argument that this multiplicity of terms is best viewed as James's sense of the chaotic, not because that is the terminology that he uses, but because as a whole they operate in a way we can best describe as chaotic. In order to understand James's sense of the chaotic more precisely, we need to take a close look at *The Principles of Psychology* and relevant biographical information, but I can anticipate somewhat by recalling the variety with which chaos and the chaotic have been used historically. A similar variety seems to exist in James, but prominent within it is the sense of the chaotic we saw in his friend, Henry Adams, and the poet who was in many senses an heir, Wallace Stevens, of a chaos that can be beneficial.

The tempestuous world: roots of the chaotic in James's crisis years, 1867-1872

Since the *Principles* was so long in the making, we need first to look backward. Gerald E. Myers points out that the thought in the *Principles* doesn't characterize merely one stage in James's thought so much as it represents a lengthy line of development.[54] That seems especially true of James's attitude toward the set of ideas that concern us here, and is a warrant for some minor excavating into James's biography.

Few summaries of childhood are more striking than Henry James's statement that "the literal played in our education as small a part as it perhaps ever played in any, and we wholesomely breathed inconsistency and ate and drank contradictions."[55] The liberal thought and whimsicality of Henry James, Sr.; the family's frequent moves and travels; the "cheerful anarchy" of the schooling of the James children; their "quickening collision" with friends of their father's such as Emerson, Thoreau, Thackery, Ripley, and many others, and with several cities in Europe—all made change and stimulation seemingly the only constants in their childhood.[56] Though William James's son, Henry, traces his father's intellectual flexibility back to the mobility of his youth, I will resist the temptation to draw conclusions too quickly from the facts of childhood, alluring though they are.[57]

The facts of young manhood are a different matter. James's physical ills and mental depression dominated his life from his bout with a mild form of smallpox in Brazil in May of 1865 until the second year of his teaching at Harvard in the early 1870s, and continued, though much abated, for the rest of his life. Commentators interpret the significance of James's illness differently. The predominant view has been that of Ralph Barton Perry who sees philosophy as the key to James's difficulties. James's depression involved questions about the nature of the world and his own nature as an agent in that world. He was unable to sort out the degree to which his restlessness and paralysis were laid upon him, whether by a physiological cause or by the oppressive character of life more generally. His profound and painful struggle of so many years' duration was toward the discovery of the efficacy of his own will. He had, as his sister Alice remarked, "a chronic infirmity of will."[58] Perry sees this personal crisis as one "that could be relieved only by a *philosophical* insight."[59] Because of James's extreme personal involvement with it, "philosophy was never a mere theory, but always a set of beliefs which reconciled him to life and which he proclaimed as one preaching a way of salvation."[60] Jacques Barzun echoes that view when he states that James philosophized "from the need to survive intellectually and emotionally."[61]

Gay Wilson Allen emphasizes a psychological interpretation of James's emotional difficulties. He sees James denying himself an affectionate and sexual relationship with women while craving such a relation at the same time. The conflict, Allen suggests, goes far toward explaining James's condition. Like Perry, he argues for the importance of the strengthening of James's will, and speaks of the value of James's teaching and ultimately his marriage to Alice Howe Gibbens for his final recovery.[62]

A somewhat provocative version comes from the psychologist Howard M. Feinstein who interprets James's emotional turmoil in terms of his internalized struggle with his father for an identity and vocation of his own. It was not James's discovery of the freedom of the will through reading Renouvier, that is, not philosophy that saved James. Rather, James had to find a way to stop stifling his desire to devote himself to art or philosophy rather than to his father's choice, science. "Instead of freedom *of* the will, William needed to be freed *from* the will," that is, his father's will. Like Allen, Feinstein feels that teaching was central to James's health. In becoming a professor of physiology and then psychology, James found a way to satisfy his own needs and the demands of his psychological heritage.[63]

A complement to Feinstein is James William Anderson who sees James's difficulty stemming from his mother rather than his father. According to this interpretation, Mary James failed to provide adequate maternal care for her son. The result was a fragile "self-structure," a sense of hollowness, and development of a "false self" to mask what he sensed to be a weak, small, needy, infantile self. James's depression, his isolation, his inability to develop autonomy were consequences of this lack of a stable self, and the difficulty was greatly solved with his marriage to Alice Gibbens who offered the empathy, admiration, and consistency that James sought.[64]

I don't propose to adjudicate among these different interpretations. Rather, I accept them all as illuminating to a great extent. My interest is not in psychological analysis but in the analysis of how James himself articulated his difficulties, in the imagery he used, because the manner in which he imagined his predicament and its resolution greatly illumines his sense of the chaotic.

Primary among his problems is what his sister Alice mildly censored as "chronic infirmity of will," or what James himself termed "deadness of spirit." James had gone off rather suddenly to Europe in the spring of 1867 after being on the verge of suicide in the winter of that year. He tried the mineral bath treatments at Teplitz but became more depressed than before, and again considered suicide. Shortly thereafter he wrote his friend Oliver Wendell Holmes, Jr., complaining of the "stagnation" of his inner life. It is the absence of "motion, excitement or life," a "deadness" that troubles James. After his return to Cambridge late in 1868, recalled by his parents rather than cured, he depicts himself in a letter to Henry as a ship dead in the water, sails furled. "What is a man to write when a reef is being taken in his existence?"[65] The French correspondent passage from the *Varieties* reveals a similar fear of utter motionlessness. He visualizes himself as a patient in an asylum:

> a black-haired youth with greenish skin, entirely idiotic, who used to sit all day on one of the benches, or rather shelves, against the wall, with his knees drawn up against his chin, and the coarse gray undershirt, which was his only garment, drawn over them, inclosing his entire figure. He sat there like a sort of sculptured Egyptian cat or Peruvian mummy, moving nothing but his black eyes and looking absolutely non-human.[66]

It is James's moment of greatest horror. He sees himself as lifeless, vegetative, mummified, catatonic, as a figure on a shelf. Perhaps James could not bring himself to fulfill his father's wishes to study science; perhaps he could not discover the place of his individual will in a deterministic universe, reconcile his craving for a fulfilling relationship with his Victorian conscience, or form a stable self. Yet the image through which he perceives himself and his position is that of paralysis.

If James's condition is paralysis, his aim must be motion, and indeed it is. Yet any motion would not do. In his letters, James speaks not only of a paralysis that oppresses but a paralysis prescribed. "Muscular and cerebral activity not only remain *unexcited*, but are *solicited*, by an idiotic hope of recovery, to crass indolence."[67] The trip to Europe in 1867-68, his shuttling between Dresden, Teplitz, and Berlin are, paradoxically enough, for rest. Like the Belgian doctor who gravely advises Marlow, "Du calme, du calme" before he departs for the heart of darkness, the latter half of the nineteenth century believed in rest. In 1866, soon after his return from the Agassiz expedition to Brazil and while he was studying medicine that he hoped he would find more interesting than he had before the year's detour, James wrote to Tom Ward. What he needs, he says, is limitation. "I am conscious of a desire I never had so strongly or so permanently, of narrowing and deepening the channel of my intellectual activity, of economizing my feeble energies and consequently treating with more respect the few things I shall devote them to."[68] What limitation can give to him is harmony and calm. They define what he terms his "salvation." He intends to imitate those who "reach a point from which the view within certain limits is harmonious, and they keep within those limits; they find as it were a centre of oscillation in which they may be at rest." From James's prescription we can see how he visualizes his problem. The matter that must be addressed through limitation produces disquiet. It is disharmonious. It is out of bounds. The image we get is of a search for a haven of safety and calm and what is fled is some tempestuousness that overwhelms. James seems caught in a chaos as Shakespeare or

Hobbes viewed it: he is in a maelstrom, a tempest.

James sees himself as stagnating and still in comparison with a world that appears to possess all power as well as dizzying, disorienting motion. In an 1870 letter to Ward, he again speaks of limitation, of "habits of order" that enable a slow but steady progression, "grain on grain of willful choice." His own purposeful motion must be tiny considering the disproportion of his power to the disorder of the world. He recalls that previously "when I have felt like taking a free initiative, like daring to act originally, without carefully waiting for contemplation of the external world to determine all for me, suicide seemed the most manly form to put my daring into."[69] It's a remarkable summary of the disproportion James saw between himself and the world, as well of that world's disorder. His self was so insignificant that his most daring act would be to surrender to the world's destructive power. The world challenges and directs, and it saps the self of originality, initiative, reality, and finally of existence. Not to act is to be swept by the world into the intellectual and emotional turmoil he had experienced through several years, which is to say, an inability to move under his own power. To dare to act is to surrender to die, that is, to submit to the destructiveness of the world, but willingly. In either case he is in a maelstrom that threatens to sweep him inexorably down to destruction.

James's other explicit references to suicide clarify his developing sense of the desirability of some sort of motion. In a letter to his father in September 1867, he speaks of his forced immobility in Dresden because of his back and of the resulting "thoughts of the pistol, the dagger and the bowl. . . . [S]ome change, even if a hazardous one, was necessary."[70] Though he speaks here of a move to Teplitz as the hazardous change, it is apparent enough that suicide is also a change preferable to his enforced repose; his inability to study physiology, as had been his plan; and his paralyzed confusion concerning his desires and abilities. Suicide does not offer rest; it offers motion. As he notes in a letter a year later, in death he sees "fermentation and crumbling and evaporation and diffusion."[71] What he emphasizes is not decay but activity, a flowing into the universe. This "step out into the green darkness" is certainly characterized more attractively than the tempestuousness he alludes to elsewhere. It is "innocent and desirable." In fact, it seems to be an early manifestation of James's great love of inclusiveness, his desire to welcome as much of the "teeming and dramatic richness" of the world as possible.[72] If James rejects the motion of suicide for the "tatters and shreds of beauty" that are interwoven with his otherwise "loathsome and grotesque" life, in part it is because he is gradually becoming able to achieve his own motion. But the ideal of perfectly fluid motion is one that remains.

James finds his way to motion, though the sort he manages is often not described as motion at all. He can gain "tatters and shreds," make a "nick," accumulate "grain on grain." But the particles and pieces add up to an action, however restricted. The grains mount up when habits of order enable us to "advance to really interesting fields of action."[73] Even resignation to the evils of the world provides "ground and leisure to advance to new philanthropic action."[74] Advance to action: the phrase indicates James's tentativeness, for though it is an emphatic military metaphor, it denies the action in the advance itself. Isn't the advance action, too? Then why *advance* to action? Nonetheless, however hesitant and partial, it is motion that James desires and motion that he gradually achieves. "We all learn sooner or later that we must gather ourselves up, and more or less arbitrarily concentrate our interests—throw much overboard to save any," he writes to Henry in 1869.[75] Though his ship is disabled and still in danger of sinking, it is afloat and limping along, like Conrad's *Patna* or *Narcissus*.

What seems to happen in the final term of these difficult but highly important years for James's thought, is a growing widening of boundaries and loosening of limits. The movement that the self can achieve is not a slow, narrow gathering of grains but becomes more expansive. It is tempting to say that the motion of the self assimilates some of the characteristics of the threatening, tempestuous world and thereby becomes able to deal with it more adequately. In some notes James writes of two kinds of self-assertion, "the expansive, embracing [and] the centripetal, defensive."[76] James wonders if the two might be combined. The great difference evident here is that it is possible for him to consider something other than sheer defense or slow, small steps; he can contemplate taking the universe in. The expansive motion is similar to that in his lyrical contemplation of suicide, the "step out into the green darkness," but here he expands and incorporates rather than dissolves. The only way he could do so, he feels, is if the mind "is so purely fluid or plastic." What a change we can see in this statement. Far from the mind being paralyzed in life and fluid only in death, James sees it flowing beyond narrow fixed limits that purely defend it and instead encompassing the universe. It's important to note that James doesn't feel he can do so at this time; important, too, to recall that the French correspondent incident takes place shortly after this, between the fall of 1869 and the spring of 1870. But the alternative to paralysis and the really successful counter to the threatening movement of the world is visualized as limitation combined with fluidity. "[Do] the two combine and give respect?" he wonders in conclusion.

What does James have in mind by the combination of limitation and fluidity? We may get our clearest idea from the "finished" James, of the later 1870s, once the depths of his crises had passed. In an article published in *The Nation* in 1876, he expresses his views on the teaching of philosophy. Its greatest value, he says, is in giving students a fluidity of mind. "Philosophic study means the habit of always seeing an alternative, of not taking the usual for granted, of making conventionalities fluid again, of imagining foreign states of mind."[77] James seems to be advocating the "mind so purely fluid or plastic" that he had mused upon in 1869. The sort of mental motion that James urges is an outward movement, toward the unknown and the indefinite; it flows around, over, or through the stable, staid, and solid. It overcomes the exclusions of the conventional, the expected, and the established. Moreover, such fluidity is possible because of its combination with limitation, as he had predicted in 1869. It is a *habit* of fluidity that James speaks of, which is to say, the fluidity is an integral part of personality. It takes place, he says, from within an "independent, personal look at all the data of life."[78]

Evidently James has come to the liberating view that movement is an integral part of self, and the nature of that movement seems remarkably similar to the tempestuousness that had hobbled and threatened him. It is a motion that overcomes limits, that challenges and dissolves the fixed and definite, whether that be the structures of James's self or the inhibiting conventions of thought. Of course, the chaos of the world, which haunted him in the late 1860s and early 1870s, was extreme and destructive. It ruptured bounds and required strict defenses. It was the traditional chaos that is utterly disorderly and threatening. The harnessed power of fluidity within operates not only more gently but also productively, as it does for Chopin, Stevens, and Adams. It seems as though James overcomes the danger of tempestuousness not, as in Poe's "Descent into the Maelstrom," by surrendering to the chaos without, but, closer to Conrad, by realizing his own, intrinsic moral resources, in this case of creative instability. He discovers a fluidity that dissolves the fixed, flows past the coercion of the conventional, moves into the strange, and is an ineluctable aspect of the self. James doesn't lose his anxiety about the tempestuous. "My strongest moral and intellectual craving is for some stable reality to lean upon," he writes in 1873.[79] But in a way he has incorporated the instability that he had feared.

What do we learn of James and the chaotic by this quick glance through his years of crisis? We see a kind of motion that threatens the self, challenging its autonomy and its ability to act, a tempestuousness that creates paralysis and necessitates defensive limitations. We also see a kind of motion that is enabling, which allows the self to overcome paralysis and to incorporate the new and the strange. Integral to personality is a motion that is inclusive and that contrasts with and challenges the fixed, the conventional, the familiar, and the external chaos of the world. This was how James imagined his predicament and his need in the 1860s and 1870s. It might be divided into the harsh chaotic without and the harnessed power of the chaotic within. Both poles are dominant in the *Principles*, as we shall see in the next chapter.

2
"A Mind So Purely Fluid": The Chaotic in *The Principles of Psychology*: Part 2

External chaos: the plenum

When James begins his study of the mind from within in his chapter on the stream of consciousness, he states his governing, empirical rule, that "the only thing which psychology has a right to postulate at the outset is the fact of thinking itself."[1] In many ways it would have been well had James followed his own dictum more strictly, not speculating about the nature of nerve physiology and its relationship to thought or the nature of the world apart from our thought of it. Yet both of these areas, and especially the second, afford us a valuable view of James's imagination.[2]

In order to highlight the role that is played by interest in consciousness, James frequently refers to the nature of the world that exists apart from interest. It is something we can neither think of nor experience, he says, since selection is so basic to consciousness. "We have no organ or faculty to appreciate the simply given order," he states.[3] Nonetheless, James does have a conception of it, and it is one that is highly consistent through the course of the *Principles*. In brief, the world apart from consciousness is characterized as a primordial soup, incredibly rich in potential objects and relations; it is the reservoir of raw materials from which humans fashion the world.

To a certain extent James seems to want to conceive of "outer reality" in purely negative terms. It is "undistinguishable . . . devoid of distinction or emphasis."[4] It is a "black and jointless continuity." But already in that second passage James is fashioning a character. The world is not just lacking the color or body that interest gives, it is the night, full of

21

"moving clouds of swarming atoms."[5] It is, above all, full, "a plenum."[6] Moreover, it is an interconnected whole, each part essential and leading to every other part, so that, "it is truly said that to know one thing thoroughly is to know the whole universe."[7] Sensation, perception, attention, discrimination, conception, and reasoning, our morality, aesthetics, and science all operate on the principle of selection, whereby some portion of the plenum is chosen according to some purpose and the rest ignored.[8] Partiality and limitation are the rule, and "outer reality" is the mine of incredible wealth that furnishes the ore for all our activities.

The plenum, then, supplies us with all that we have of the world. In a telling figure, James speaks of our minds as operating like sculptors, fashioning our consciousness from the marble of reality. The metaphor emphasizes not only the nature of the world as a source, but the variety of products possible. "There were a thousand different [statues] beside it, and the sculptor alone is to thank for having extricated this one from the rest. . . . Other sculptors, other statues from the same stone! Other minds, other worlds from the same monotonous and inexpressive chaos!"[9] James tends to use expressions of multiplicity when emphasizing that the plenum exceeds our fragmentations of it. There is an "infinite chaos of movements" from which sense selects.[10] That which is ignored by particular interests remains, and in some sense it calls upon us to do it greater justice, to break out from partiality.

Finally there is something inhuman about the "infinite chaos." It is something "with which we have nothing to do but to get away from it as fast as possible."[11] It offers us a "more," but it also offers too much, necessitating a protective filtering that recalls the limitation that was of such importance to James's thought in his years of crisis. Our "mental sanity" depends on most of the "utter chaos of actual experience" becoming nonexistent.[12]

James clearly says more of the plenum than his own thought allows. If we are limited to what we directly experience, then we have no knowledge whatsoever of the world aside from our experience of it. In this James is far closer to

Kant than he knew or might have wanted to acknowledge. It is certainly legitimate to speculate about what the world must be like for our experience of it to be as it is, but there is a considerable range of speculation possible. James sometimes goes for the minimum, as when he speaks of sameness. That is, he does not care whether there be "real sameness in things or not. . . . Real sameness might rain down upon us from the outer world . . . [or] the outer world might be an unbroken flux." All that matters is an intention to think the same.[13] Similarly, he terms it "the miracle of miracles" that the purely human constructs of science are supported by reality.[14] At the other extreme, he argues that time and space relations exist in the world and our knowledge of them is impressed from without. "The mind is passive and tributary, a servile copy, fatally and unresistingly fashioned from without [in its knowledge of] such truths as that fire burns and water wets, that glass refracts, heat melts snow, fishes live in water and die on land, and the like."[15]

Voltaire considered all metaphysical speculation to compound the evil it pretended to explain. "*Non liquet*, it's not clear," were the words he wanted to append to every chapter of speculation.[16] James may have distrusted Hegelian and neo-Kantian philosophy, but he is not a skeptic, and he usually opts for more than the minimum in considering what the world must be like to produce our experience.[17] It is not entirely clear just what picture he has of that world. As Charlene Haddock Seigfried points out, James is inconsistent, sometimes asserting a chaotic world that we must order ourselves and at other times a reality that is ordered and must be passively received. She reconciles the two tendencies in a "quasi-chaos" that contains a multiplicity of relations, some of which are realized in particular contexts and others in other contexts.[18] So relations are real and exist in the world, but we are not the merely passive beings James asserts toward the end of the *Principles*. This seems a characterization James might well have agreed with, and it underscores the degree to which James's imagination found ideas of the chaotic to be congenial. When he speculates what reality must be like to produce the inner life that he introspects, he imagines a swirling primordial chaos that is rich, demanding, and vaguely threatening. It is not a vastly different depiction from the one we've seen figuring in his years of crisis, and it is one that he does not drop in entering the inner world.

A circumscription of the chaotic

Before I turn to the internal chaos involved in the stream of consciousness, it would be helpful to look, once again, at the nature of chaos. In the first chapter I argued that chaos is usually used negatively, to indicate what is *missing*, be that a hierarchy, an orderly progression, or a harmony, as in Pascal's exclamation: "What a chimera then is man! What a novelty! What a monster, what a chaos, what a contradiction, what a prodigy!" I also argued that a chaos is always a "chaosmos," to quote Joyce, for, paradoxically enough, the unformed must have a form. So chaos is a war, a confused mixture, even a lump. That discussion indicates how chaos is presented, but it does not tell us what chaos is. It does not offer a definition of *chaos* or the *chaotic*. As we enter more closely into the internal and external worlds that James describes, we need to know how to recognize the chaotic. What precisely is it? What do Shakespeare's emotional anguish; Hobbes's civil strife; Stevens's lazy, unregulated island life; and Adams's fecundity have in common?

There is a great deal of variety in the chaotic, so much that it requires a very inclusive definition. We can see this wide range just in what we've noted about James thus far. Reviewing James's young manhood, we isolated a conception of a tumultuous and destructive world that impersonally battered his ability to act effectively and offered him the alternatives of paralysis or death. An apt metaphor seemed to be that of the maelstrom, which was chaotic by being antithetical to the orderings necessary for life. Coexisting with that sense and growing stronger as James grew older was a sense of creative flux, the ability of a personality to incorporate a fluidity that would allow him to dissolve limitations and act successfully in the world. Though it might seem like a contradiction considering the more austere and violent sense of chaos, we termed this an integrated and domesticated chaos, which is chaotic, again, by its ability to flow around or through boundaries and limitations. As in Stevens, Chopin, and Adams, where restriction is the problem, a force that loosens restriction can be beneficial.

The *Principles* presents us with yet other images of the chaotic. The outer world loses most—though not all—of its threatening character, and seems to take on much the character of a Timaean *kaos*, a roiling caldron of raw materials from which the demiurge self constructs its world according to a high plan. As in the maelstrom, this chaos impinges on James, but in this case it is because it is a fullness beyond our structures, a wealth that mocks our limited constructions, so it stimulates rather than paralyzes.

What, then, is chaos? What do all of these examples, from James and others, have in common? Unfortunately, few scholars have dealt with the chaotic, so we can find little guidance in previous work. The writings of Samuel Beckett and Thomas Pynchon stimulated discussions of chaos, and it is worth taking a quick look at them. In a 1961 interview by Tom F. Driver, Beckett spoke of the need that art admit into itself what he variously calls "the mess," "confusion," and "chaos."[19] Beckett declares:

> The confusion is not my invention. We cannot listen to a conversation for five minutes without being acutely aware of the confusion. It is all around us and our only chance now is to let it in. The only chance of renovation is to open our eyes and see the mess. It is not a mess you can make sense of.[20]

In some part Beckett traces the lineage of "the mess" back to William James, for one synonym is "this buzzing confusion," an evident reference to James's well-known "blooming, buzzing confusion," and an indication of the degree to which James's thought comes to be associated with the *chaotic*, even though he does not often use the term. But it is also evident that Beckett's sense of the chaotic will not do as a general definition. One commentator on Beckett, David H. Hesla, defines Beckett's chaos as "the absurdity of human existence," and he clarifies the absurd as the "unnameable or unintelligible—unnameable because unintelligible, unintelligible because unnameable. The absurd is impervious to the human Logos, to human speech and reason."[21] Another critic, Raymond Federman, equates chaos with meaninglessness and disintegration.[22] While such a sense of chaos is certainly the heir of the views of utter disorder and confusion that I have discussed, it also has become something peculiar to the twentieth century and allied to existentialism. Such a generalization will not do for our purposes because it is too particular historically and it comes from but one end of the continuum of the chaotic.

Quite a few critics responded to Pynchon's writings in the 1960s and 1970s with a new critical tool, the notion of *entropy*.[23] The term is drawn from the second law of thermodynamics, the first law of which states that energy can never be created or destroyed, only transformed. The second law adds that there is a decrease in available energy with each transformation. Such a decrease is an increase in entropy. So when wood is burned and heat, light, and ash result, those products contain less available energy. They are less concentrated, less organized, and more random: in a word, there is greater entropy. The final result of all energy transformations in a closed system is perfect entropy or energy death. In writing of entropy, the most commonly used synonyms are disorder and chaos.

As with any notion of chaos, this one has a particular form. One way to picture entropy is as a perfect distribution of molecules, all with the identical energy level. If all the energetic molecules were in one place, energy could flow to less energetic molecules. But a perfect distribution of molecules with identical energy would be a perfect equilibrium and no energy transfers could take place. This would be perfect entropy or chaos. It is a somewhat interesting use of chaos. It is certainly not the Miltonic idea of warring elements or any of the other concepts of chaos we've discussed. As Peter L. Abernethy says, "Disorder and chaos, then, do not mean a random jumble of things but rather uniformity, a lack of distinctions, a sameness, a lack of individuality, a tendency toward complete conformity."[24] So the chaos of entropy is not war but stasis.[25]

This use of chaos supports my argument that chaos can take many forms: there is chaos and there is chaos. At base, entropy concerns energy, but by extension it has to do with the conditions necessary for energy. This entropic chaos is a condition where there is less structure, order, and form, and therefore less energy. In particular, it is used to contrast with organization. Those who speak of chaos in this sense have their eyes on comparatively complex structures that can only diminish in their complexity as time goes by and become more random and uniform. That result they call entropy and chaos. In this, somewhat modern view, chaos is motionless-ness; it is death. Milton, on the other hand, is not interested in randomness or uniformity but in what is not harmonious or hierarchically structured. His chaos is anarchy, an utter jumble of warring elements. In the modern view, where energy and change have value, chaos is stillness; whereas the traditional view that valued stability saw chaos as uncontrol-lable change.[26] But entropy is not what Shakespeare and Stevens, Pascal and Adams, Ovid and Beckett, or the several faces of William James all have in common when they speak of chaos. It seems to add yet one more form of this multi-formed formlessness.

Yet another use of chaos comes from the scientific com-munity. In the 1970s and 1980s there has been an abundance of research into chaos theory, summarized and popularized by James Gleick's *Chaos: Making a New Science*. As he states, "[Classical science] had suffered a special ignorance about disorder in the atmosphere, in the turbulent sea, in the fluctuations of wildlife populations, in the oscillations of the heart and brain. The irregular side of nature, the discontinu-ous and erratic side—these have been puzzles to science, or worse, monstrosities." In these investigations, chaos seems to be synonymous with extreme complexity, beyond the ordi-nary capacity of science to simplify and comprehend. Usual synonyms are "unpredictability," "randomness," "wildness," "disorder," "instability," "irregularity," "discontinuity," and "richness." It is certainly a different usage than that in entropy. It reveals the concern with what chaos is not—not the usual predictability, regularity, and stability that the Newtonian and Einsteinian universe display—and it communicates that lack through the image of a rather Miltonic tumultuousness, though one viewed positively. As Gleick notes, "Articles on chaos from the late 1970s onward sounded evangelical. . . . The disorderly behavior of simple systems acted as a creative process. It generated complexity: richly organized patterns . . . with the fascination of living things." My argument that the formless has form is supported by these scientists who are so excited about chaos because they find order in it.[27] But neither Gleick nor the chaos scientists offer a definition of *chaos*; they provide yet another use of the term.

Neither Beckett, entropy, nor Gleick solves our problem by offering a general sense of chaos that can encompass all the uses we have surveyed. My own suggestion is this: if we ask what seems to be constant in all these chaoses, I believe we find a contrast to something else that is, in some sense, more ordered, structured, or formed. The chaotic is *relative*, and in two senses: there are many degrees of it, that is to say, it can be "utter" or not so utter. And it is always relative to some order that it both lacks and, in some sense, challenges. So during James's crisis years, the world issued a severe challenge to his fragile sense of self. It threatened to tear apart his weak structures of identity and purpose. In the somewhat later James, the inquisitive and fluid mind sought to break down protective limitations. Compared to the defensive structures that he had built, and to the established forms of conventional wisdom, James's curiosity and desire to take in all he ran across was chaotic. Finally, the elements of the plenum not only lack the distinctness of human concepts and sensations, but they exert some sort of a pressure on them toward greater adequacy.

This relative sense of chaos that I am offering may seem weak for the more vigorous uses of chaos, but we must take account of the full spectrum of the chaotic and not be distracted by the more extreme uses. My characterization gathers together a concept that exists in many different forms in James, as it does in the Western tradition, and we cannot see just how widespread and varied it is in James without an adequately comprehensive understanding of it. So, to repeat, the chaotic involves a contrast and challenge to something else that is, in some sense, more ordered, structured, or formed.

Internal chaos: the stream

If there is a chaos without, there is also a chaos within, and to a far greater extent than was evident in our look at the biographical documents. In fact, the inner and outer realms are analogous in the *Principles*.[28] Looking at consciousness, what we find, "from our natal day, is a teeming multiplicity of objects and relations" that sounds like the "infinite chaos of movements" that characterizes the "outer world."[29] Yet while the two realms are analogous, James tells us much more about consciousness since that is the focus of the bulk of the two volumes.

In brief, consciousness has five characteristics, each of which is involved in its general chaotic character: consciousness is continuous, always changing, always part of a personality, interested in some parts of these objects and not in others, and it "appears to deal with objects independent of itself."[30]

Continuity

The first aspect, continuity, suggests to James the highly influential metaphor of the stream. In looking at our own minds, what we perceive is not a chain or a train, "nothing jointed," but rather a flow of consciousness.[31] Of course, what we perceive is not the monotonous and seamless continuum of the hypothetical plenum. There are thoughts and sensations that mark differences within the stream. But the discontinuities of content are contained within the continuity of the flow. So in James's striking example, a clap of thunder does not absolutely break in upon silence to be succeeded by a discrete silence once again. We do not have "grain on grain" of consciousness. It is more fluid than that. "Into the awareness of the thunder itself the awareness of the previous silence creeps and continues; for what we hear when the thunder crashes is not thunder *pure*, but thunder-breaking-upon-silence-and-contrasting-with-it."[32]

As the plenum was characterized by innumerable connections, each part leading to every other, so the vast volume of the stream is relational. The continuity of consciousness comes from such relations. James divides consciousness into substantives and transitives, definite mental resting places, and the means by which we move on to other definite thoughts or sensations. He offers two illuminating metaphors for this observation, one linguistic and one natural. The substantives of thought are the nouns, but James insists that it is not nouns alone that reflect our thought; rather all the other parts of speech reflect consciousness as well.

> There is not a conjunction or a preposition, and hardly an adverbial phrase, syntactic form, or inflection of voice, in human speech, that does not express some shading or other of relation which we at some moment actually feel to exist between the larger objects of our thought.[33]

The natural figure is that of the perching and flying bird, its flight being the movements of our thought, and its comparatively briefer perchings being the substantives.

Both metaphors express the importance of the relational aspects of consciousness, the greater quantity of them when compared to substantives, and the continuity that flows among and between the more evident definite thoughts and sensations. Though both metaphors are striking and helpful, the bird metaphor being especially evocative,[34] the figure James uses most widely is that of the "fringe." The fringe spreads out in all directions from any definite thought, and is composed of "the sense of [the thought's] relations near and remote, the dying echo of whence it came to us, the dawning sense of whither it is to lead."[35] In the chapter on the stream of consciousness, James offers a number of examples of the fringe. There are "feelings of tendency," the sense of expectancy when we await an impression in response to a called, "Look!" or when we try to recall a name. He also speaks of the "sense of affinity," the feeling about thoughts that they will or will not further the solution of a problem when that solution only exists as a gap in our minds.[36]

The rest of the *Principles* presents innumerable other ways in which the fringe operates. In fact, there are few chapters where we do not find a significant reference to the fringe, for it is one of James's central insights and controlling ideas. For example, the difference between sensation and perception is purely a matter of the presence or absence of the fringe. Pure sensation, the function whereby infants become aware of the "bare immediate natures" of objects with no knowledge of their relations to other objects, lacks a fringe. Adults inevitably assimilate a sensation to what is already known. An object is "classed, located, measured, compared, assigned to a function, etc., etc."[37] Perception, then, is educated, not innocent, and to it clings the fringe of all other perceptions of that kind, memories of such perceptions, expectations of the consequences that have followed and might now. All perception is apperception according to this view; a fringe sits already formed for each sensation; each is already immersed in the "free water" of consciousness.

Memory, too, involves the fringe, since what is involved in memory is not the mere reproduction of an object or event. What is remembered "[must] be expressly referred to the past." We do that by associating the recollection with a date or event. Moreover, the memory must have the "warmth and intimacy" that identify it as one's own.[38] Thus, any memory is surrounded with a fringe of relations that alone enable it to be a memory.

The section of the *Principles* that offers the most valuable information about the fringe is the chapter on association. It presents the laws of the flowing of the stream, of the transitions among substances, of the flights between perchings, of the structure of the fringe. James even speaks of the "mechanical conditions" of association, which he traces to the "law of neural habit."[39] Yet if James speaks of the lawfulness of the stream, surely I must be mistaken in saying the chaotic has anything to do with it, for if chaos contrasts with anything, it is with law. Yet, as I indicated in chapter 1, there is no strict antithesis between chaos and order: the unformed has a form; the disorderly has an order. And as I indicated earlier in the present chapter, all that is required for the chaotic is a *contrast* to something that is more ordered, structured, or formed. The structures that are challenged by the continuity of consciousness are the "substantives" of consciousness, the discrete objects and states upon which psychology traditionally focuses. The notion of the stream submerges such "definite images" within the "free water" of consciousness: the feelings of tendency and expectancy, associated objects and states, and the relation to the past and to the self that inevitably accompany any substantives. The "chaotic fringe" dissolves discreteness in "numberless" relations,[40] so instead of remaining within strict limits, a thought spreads off into far reaches of consciousness.

There are still other chaotic aspects to James's treatment of the continuity of consciousness. He speaks of his desire to reinstate "the vague" to its proper place in mental life, and certainly vagueness tends to conceal sharp boundaries as a kind of mist and so might be seen as a functioning of the chaotic.[41] In addition, not only is there less definiteness because of the fringe, but the fringe itself, the transitive aspect of thought, is fragile, subtle, easily eclipsed: it is "always on the wing, so to speak, and not to be glimpsed except in flight."[42] So it is in its very nature to resist capture. "Let anyone try to cut a thought across in the middle and get a look at its section, and he will see how difficult the introspective observation of the transitive tracts is."[43]

The lawfulness of the stream is also mitigated by the chaos of vagueness and indeterminacy. Habit, recency, vividness, and emotional congruity may combine to make a particular association likely, but "it still must be confessed that an immense number of terms in the linked chain of our representations fall outside of all assignable rule."[44] James hopes that "possibly a minute insight into the laws of neural action will some day clear the matter up," but one senses that he would not be entirely pleased to have a clear and succinct book of rules. In *Talks to Teachers* he considers the accusation that he might hold "a mechanical and even a materialist view of the mind," and affirms his belief that indeterminacy plays a far too important role in thought for that to be true.[45] Moreover, he argues that indeterminacy actually saves species from considerable danger, particularly when contrasted with mechanical responses, and he offers a typically vivid illustration.

> Frogs and toads . . . show . . . a machine-like obedience to the present incitement of sense, and an almost total exclusion of the power of choice. Copulation occurs *per fas aut nefas*, occasionally between males, often with dead females, in puddles exposed on the highway. . . . Every spring an immense sacrifice of batrachian life takes place from these causes alone.[46]

Humans' actions are not determinable, however minutely neural action may be examined, and it is the very vagueness of their possibilities, the absence of mechanical predictability that saves them from such "immense sacrifice." James would not want to "clear the matter up" with a complete set of determining laws of the movement of the stream because he would lose the benefits of chaos.

Change

So the continuity of consciousness gives it a chaotic character, yet, to repeat, it is not a sheer continuity but one containing discontinuity within itself. For the second characteristic of consciousness is that it is constantly changing. James's intention in discussing this aspect of the mind is to disprove the theory of "simple ideas," which is found in Locke and others. He disagrees with the notion that all states of consciousness are the result of various combinations of certain basic sensations that themselves do not change. James's alternative is based on his notion that consciousness is a whole, not a compound. Such a whole cannot recur for several reasons, among them that circumstances change, which means that our sensibility is altered, and that the fringe of any thought or perception is new. "When the identical fact recurs, we *must* think of it under a somewhat different angle, apprehend it in different relations from those in which it last appeared."[47] Thus, our consciousness is not composed of identical pieces, formed by objects. If anything changes, if the stream flows at all, the entire river is different, as is each section of it.

Yet another consequence of change, one that James does not deal with directly, is that our consciousness is of multiplicity. James approves Shadworth Hodgson's words that "What I find, when I look at my consciousness at all . . . is a sequence of different feelings. . . . The chain of consciousness is a sequence of *differents*."[48] James adds, "Now we are seeing, now hearing; now reasoning, now willing; now recollecting, now expecting; now loving, now hating."[49] If consciousness constantly changes, it is constantly different, and that is evident as a multiplicity of states.

The affinity between multiplicity and the chaotic is seen in a number of ways. James represents the "simply given order" of the plenum as a "sum." "While I talk and the flies buzz, a sea-gull catches a fish at the mouth of the Amazon, a tree falls in the Adirondack wilderness, a man sneezes in Germany, a horse dies in Tartary, and twins are born in France."[50] Even in consciousness, chaos is represented as a multiplicity. In the movement from the plenum toward full consciousness, the first step is "the chaos of fragmentary impressions interrupting each other."[51] Full consciousness is of a "teeming multiplicity."[52] When an individual has few interests with which to structure experience, there results an "extreme mobility of attention," such that "the child seem[s] to belong less to himself than to every object which happens to capture his notice."[53] The relations that constitute the free water of consciousness are "numberless." An individual has as many selves as there are people who recognize him or her.[54] The examples are themselves legion.

There is multiplicity everywhere we look in James. It seems to be a barometer of the chaotic. Nothing is single or unified; nothing is alone, discrete, unchanging. Instead, all is many. The mind, like the universe he discusses in *Pragmatism*, is a multiverse. Everything dissolves into a dozen things—or, better, an indeterminate number of things. In speaking of the "simply given order," James himself uses multiplicity to communicate the sheer fullness of the plenum. That seems to be a central aspect of its chaotic nature. I take the presence of multiplicity throughout James's discussions of consciousness in all its aspects as an indication of a similar fullness and as an indication of the chaotic. The multiplicity that exists in continuity and change is a means for James to express both that relations are numberless and that the new constantly arises. In both cases multiplicity is a device that challenges the single, the discrete, and the still. And that, as we've seen, is the best sense we can make of the chaotic.

Personality

Of all the philosophers in the modern period, it is hard to think of one for whom personality meant more than it did for James. "Imagine entirely leaving out the human in a history of literature!" he lamented after writing one of his first book reviews.[55] It is a theme that runs through his writings, perhaps most notably in his view of the importance of temperament for philosophy. "Pretend what we may, the whole man within us is at work when we form our philosophical opinions. Intellect, will, taste, and passion co-operate just as they do in practical affairs."[56] James certainly did not leave personality out of the *Principles*, populating the textbook with an immense cast of characters, and making personality one of the characteristics of consciousness.

Multiplicity and the fringe combine in personality. James isn't very clear about what he means when he says that "every thought tends to be part of a personal consciousness."[57] He says only that we identify our thoughts as our own. "The universal conscious fact is not 'feelings and thoughts exist,' but 'I think' and 'I feel.'"[58] Yet he seems to mean more than a minimal identification. Rather, he feels that consciousness has personality in a full sense. He sees cases of spiritualism, hypnotism, and hysteria as forming genuine, "secondary personal selves," and describes them as "organized selves with a memory, habits, and sense of their own identity."[59] What he speaks of would seem to add substance to the "I" in "'I think' and 'I feel.'" It indicates that thoughts for James seem to have a fringe that connects them to the full blood of personality; that any thought or utterance is indelibly a personal thought or utterance.

I don't wish to argue that the existence of personality is chaotic, at least I hope I don't. But James doesn't drop the matter after coupling consciousness with personality. He quickly moves to the existence of multiple selves. There are the somewhat occult and clinical cases of "secondary personal selves," but more common and more significant is the "stream of selves."[60] He argues that the self is constituted of material, social, and spiritual selves. The first two, in particular, are multiple. Our material self is defined by the objects that are ours. Should something happen to one of those objects, our home, a manuscript, our clothes, then our self is affected. This is because it is hard to distinguish between what is "me" and what is "mine." "In the widest possible sense . . . a man's Self is the sum total of all that he can call his."[61] Similarly, we have as many social selves as social relationships. "We do not show ourselves to our children as to our club companions, to our customers as to the laborers we employ, to our own masters and employers as to our intimate friends."[62] The spiritual self is not multiple, but it adds a self to the others mentioned. James does not so much define this self as circumscribe it, much as he does religion in the *Varieties*. In general it seems to be the active self, the self that takes interest, thus engaging with the world and making it into the sort of world it is for an individual through attention, perception, conception, discrimination, imagination, emotion, and will.[63] It seems to be what James was struggling to realize in his own life during the late 1860's and early 1870's: a self that was fluid enough to take the world in and mold it within the limitations of personality.

The existence of the "stream of selves" is sufficient to indicate yet another instance of the chaotic nature of consciousness for James. In addition, the selves are often in conflict. Not all of the selves can be realized in actual circumstances, and some can be mutually exclusive.

> Not that I would not, if I could, be both handsome and fat and well-dressed, and a great athlete, and make a million a year, be a wit, a *bon-vivant*, and a lady-killer, as well as a philosopher; a philanthropist, statesman, warrior, and African explorer, as well as "tone-poet" and saint. But the thing is simply impossible.[64]

In true Jamesian fashion, one chooses those that one will pursue, and that choice determines which selves and hence which values are real and which are not.

James mentions two extremes in this definition of self: the number of selves can either be severely limited in a protective manner or it can be expanded. The question of inclusiveness is a theme that occurs frequently in James and will be treated later. For now it is only necessary to note that the stream of selves can either be damned by a Jamesian corps of engineers or it can flow deep and broad.

> All narrow people *intrench* their Me, they *retract* it—from the region of what they cannot securely possess. . . . Sympathetic people, on the contrary, proceed by the entirely opposite way of expansion and inclusion. The outline of their self often gets uncertain enough, but for this the spread of its content more than atones.[65]

It is not difficult to see where James's own sympathies lie: with more selves, a wider stream, a more inclusive, if more ill-defined and chaotic self. And perhaps we can hear a final triumph over his old paralysis in his affirmation of Marcus Aurelius. "He who, with Marcus Aurelius, can truly say, 'O Universe, I wish all that thou wishest,' has a self from which every trace of negativeness and obstructiveness has been removed—no wind can blow except to fill its sails."[66] He has moved a great distance from "throw[ing] much overboard to save any," and the terrors of the maelstrom.

Interest

The fourth characteristic of consciousness is that it is more interested in some parts of its object than in others.[67] To a great extent, this is the aspect of consciousness that pushes against chaos, for we do not live in an "infinite chaos of movements" because, in one of James's figures, we "break" it into those aspects that suit our interests. Moreover, there is a progression of mental activities, each of which narrows the relative multiplicity of the previous through the operation of interest. So sensation "make[s] for us, by attending to this motion and ignoring that, a world full of contrasts, of sharp accents, of abrupt changes, of picturesque light and shade."[68] But from that still wide range, attention must choose and ignore.[69] Attention ranges from being passive to being active, which is equivalent to being wide or narrow. When a schoolchild is called by, and attends to every object seen or heard, attention may be nearly as wide as sensation. But when we are intent to catch a very faint sensation, interest narrows the world to a sharp focal point.[70] Unless James is recommending distraction to us, he would seem to be pointing to the need for limitation in attention, to the need to defeat multiplicity.

Reasoning narrows, too, for it chooses from an "infinity of aspects or properties" those that are useful in representing an object or idea. "The mind selects . . . it chooses certain of the sensations to represent the thing most *truly*, and considers the rest as its appearances."[71] So a piece of paper is a surface for writing if one wants to pen a letter, a combustible material if starting a fire is the interest, and an example of an American industrial product if economics is the topic. Conception, too, operates against the chaotic. For James, conception is the intention to think of something as unchanging, as the same, when our experience, as we have said, is entirely of change. In conception we "[single] out some one part of the mass of matter-for-thought which the world presents, and [hold] fast to it, without confusion."[72] Our interest in this lies in being able to hold firm to objects and ideas, making not only reasoning but coherent experience possible for us.[73]

But while interest seems to be the characteristic of consciousness that most actively strives against multiplicity, it also incorporates chaotic aspects. It illustrates well my claim that the chaotic is simply ubiquitous in James. To put it briefly, James displays a preference for a multiplicity of interests. Attention, conception, and reasoning may prune the bloom of the chaotic, but they operate best when they then cultivate its luxuriant growth domestically. The most successful sort of attention, sustained attention, is not narrow. It runs on the great wealth of interests that a person brings to a topic. James clearly admires those capable of it. "In such minds, subjects bud and sprout and grow. At every moment, they please by a new consequence and rivet the attention afresh."[74] It is because such individuals are interested in so much that their attention is so lasting. Mere voluntary attention can only be maintained for a short period because of the sheer effort required, but sustained attention lasts because one's interests carry attention.[75] It lasts because it is both active and passive. Aspects of whatever is considered, a forest, a novel, or a crowd, are found interesting and spark further interests, so thoughtful consideration flowers. "Their ideas coruscate, every subject branches infinitely before their fertile minds, and so for hours they may be rapt."[76] The mind is a world to such individuals, and they are passive to the bright objects of its interests. So the most fruitful attention is one that is both active and passive, is sustained by a multitude of interests, and constantly produces surprises.

Reasoning, too, thrives when it incorporates multiplicity, though it may require exclusion to operate at all, for the most powerful reasoning is characterized by inclusiveness. James isolates two processes in reasoning: first, some aspect is chosen from an entire phenomenon to represent it; second, that aspect suggests consequences more obviously than the original phenomenon did.[77] So when considering the purchase of a piece of cloth, one may perceive that the dye is of a kind that commonly fades and makes the cloth a poor choice. Of all the characteristics of the cloth, the dye is selected, and it suggests consequences applicable to the cloth as a whole. The decision not to buy the cloth is, then, a reasoned judgment. On one level, it is limitation that is most valuable in such a process; since any object has so many aspects, we would get lost among them unless we selected. But James points out that a strong reasoner must be able to extract the right aspect to represent an object, and such sagacity requires a great variety of interests. "Now a creature which has few instinctive impulses, or interests practical or aesthetic, will dissociate few characters, and will, at best, have limited reasoning powers; while one whose interests are very varied will reason much better."[78] If our only interest is the dye, then we might buy an exceedingly ugly cloth. The more widely one's mind is able to range, the greater one's experience and the more varied one's interests, the more valuable will be the conclusions drawn. "Highly gifted minds . . . spontaneously [collect] analogous instances [and unite], in a moment what in nature the whole breadth of space and time keeps separate."[79]

Limitation is essential to reasoning, but the most valuable conclusions are reached by one whose mind is most fluid, who contains much of the world's variety within him or herself, and is able to range widely and reason creatively. In fact, we get the sense from reading James that the ideal would be the individual able to incorporate the full complexity of the universe. In 1870, on a day when James wrote in his diary that he "about touched bottom," he wondered if one could ever have a mind "so purely fluid and plastic" to be able to sympathize with the total process of the universe.[80] It seemed a far wish in 1870, but by the 1880s, he not only decided that it was possible, he made it a basic quality of the mind. It's one of many indications that the *Principles* is a work of strength and of health, a work that triumphs over paralysis and limitation by assigning great powers of fluidity to the mind. And the strength of the mind consists in its domesticated chaos.

Objects

The final characteristic of consciousness also runs counter to the chaotic, by moving toward the definite and distinct. "Human thought appears to deal with objects independent of itself," James states. It is sameness that is the basis of our belief in objects, for many people and ourselves at various times seem to have the same object of thought.[81] Sameness is, then, the anchor preventing the drift into subjectivity or utter variety.

Yet after a brief treatment of sameness, James quickly moves to topics involving a great deal less certainty and distinctness. Each seems to suggest a more chaotic nature to this aspect of consciousness. In its habitual adult state, the mind is not only conscious that objects lie before it, it knows that it knows them. But James does not allow such clarity to remain for long, moving immediately to a "primitive" or "primordial" consciousness of objects, such as takes place under the influence of anaesthetics. The state seems a great deal like James's description of the plenum. He quotes an account of "absolute psychic annihilation" that moves toward "a vague, limitless, infinite feeling." Another is of a "uniform misty background" and "a constant sound or whirr." A third describes "an undisturbed empty quiet everywhere."[82] All sound like the "gray chaotic indiscriminateness" that characterizes the outer world that has not been divided by interest.[83] So at its most primitive level, the awareness of objects is the awareness of the plenum, that is, of sheer chaos.

But even at a more sophisticated level, James dissolves distinctness. He argues that the object of a thought is its entire content, not a collection of elements or a central "kernel." In effect, he means that the object of a thought is an entire section of the stream, including the free water of the fringe: if we would refer to the object of a thought we must "name its delicate idiosyncrasy . . . with every word fringed and the whole sentence bathed in that original halo of obscure relations, which, like a horizon, then spread about its meaning."[84] Far from the object of a thought being a physical object, or even a distinct, "same" intentional object, it is a handful of psychic water, spilling from any sure grasp.

As I mentioned earlier, chaos is relative. Few would immediately identify water as chaotic, yet Novalis terms it "sensitive chaos" *(das sensible Chaos)*[85] and we can see that it is chaotic in comparison with a well-delineated physical object, or a distinct, Lockean idea. Sure structure becomes lost in water's flow. There are no edges, no outline, no firmness. So this object of thought contrasts with something more ordered. In addition, it challenges such order, at least in the *Principles*, for James intentionally refers to more ordered notions of the object in order to dissolve them in his own, more chaotic concept.

The relationship of inner to outer chaos

I mentioned at the start of this section that the chaos of the inner world is analogous to that of the outer, and I think we can see now exactly how that is so. What James variously calls "reality" and the "outer world" is a rich whirl of raw materials in which we cannot live, but that not only enables us to live but stimulates us constantly to live better by making our constructions more adequate to its fullness. It is chaotic by contrasting with the more ordered world we make, and by challenging that order. Consciousness is that more ordered world: it breaks the plenum with its interests, limits it with attention, fixes it with conception, divides it with reasoning, cements it with personality. But consciousness oscillates between the creation of boundaries and their dissolution. The "substantives" of our consciousness have a fringe that extends out of sight in all directions. The laws of association end in indeterminacy. The personality that adheres to all our thoughts is a stream of selves that conflict among themselves. Interest, which fuels attention, conception, and reason and breaks the world, works best if multiple, approximating the complexity of that world. Thought is conscious of objects independent of itself, but the distinctness of those objects dissolves in a plenumlike primitive consciousness or in the flow of the thought's entire content. The limiting and defining aspects of consciousness coexist and interact with the expanding and fluid aspects of consciousness, making the mind a microcosm of the relation of mind and world—or, more truly, making James's notion of the relation of mind and world a macrocosm of the consciousness he so acutely observes.

The neural stream

If James is drawn to water, like one of Melville's water-gazers, his fascination with the stream of consciousness is approached only by his attachment to the network of neurological currents. There are few who read the *Principles* for its accounts of nerve physiology. Most probably read around them. Yet the nerve currents course throughout this large work both because they are vestiges of James's involvement with physiological experimentation and anatomy and because they appeal so strongly to his imagination.

The law of the nerve stream is habit, a structure of fluidity. Habit is that successful blend of movement within bounds that James sought in his crisis years. It is defined by its consistency and its fluidity. Habit "simplifies the movements required to achieve a given result, makes them more accurate and diminishes fatigue."[86] Without habit we would consciously have to attend to every step of an activity, and the result, James says, would be "sorry plight."[87] Instead, all the steps involved are "fused into a continuous stream," so that the minimum of effort, attention, and error are involved. Habitual actions flow as smoothly as instinctive actions. So, "the marksman sees the bird, and, before he knows it, he has aimed and shot."[88]

It is the plasticity of nerves that enables them to have both structure and fluidity. They have "the possession of a structure weak enough to yield to an influence, but strong enough not to yield all at once."[89] Nerves are stream-bed and stream, vessel and fluid, and their plasticity consists in their ability to become streambeds when they hadn't been before, and then to continue in that form until an extraordinary cause requires that a new channel be cut. James invokes the neural stream in nearly every chapter in the two volumes, and he has extended discussions of it in the chapters on habit, sensation, perception, association, memory, imagination, hallucination, emotion, and volition. All involve the same hydrologic model.

But what is chaotic about this network? All instances of the chaotic that we have looked at so far—the outer world of the crisis years, the plenum, the stream of consciousness—we have termed *chaotic* because they contrast with and challenge other, more ordered aspects of life or mind. The neural stream does neither since there is nothing else on the neurological level. It is not analogous to the stream of consciousness that both limits and dissolves. Rather this stream is basic; it is a fluidity underlying all else. All mental life floats upon water.

If the neural stream does contrast with anything more structured, it is with what might have been neurologically—and what often is, in conscious life: a distinct and discrete sequence in thought or action that would produce ponderousness and plodding. All habit, including neural habit, avoids the effort, attention, and error that attend decision. Instead of a laborious, step-by-step progression from sensation to action, which at the most absurd level would involve deliberation at each nerve synapse, action results at once. "A glance at the musical hieroglyphics, and the pianist's fingers have rippled through a cataract of notes."[90] The real alternative to the neural stream is paralysis, James's old fear from the late 1860s. The movement that James sought in those days he discovers in our most basic physical makeup. We cannot be catatonic, wrapped in a blanket on a shelf, because our very nerves stream along, producing action effortlessly and accurately.

So like the stream of consciousness, the neural stream is domesticated: it is incorporated within us, invariably productive, and lies within relatively narrow bounds. Which is all a way of saying that this stream flows within banks. Nerve impulses do not flow just anywhere: there is not a general and indiscriminate flooding. The stream is orderly, moving from the "most drainable to the most draining cells" according to rather strict hydrological laws.[91]

But the neural stream differs from consciousness in that it does not function chaotically. There are no continuities, changes, or multiplicities that exert pressure on substantives, stases, or apparent unities and challenge them. As a result, the neural process seems less chaotic. But its fluidity reveals James's preoccupation with the chaotic to a level as fundamental physically as the stream of consciousness is psychically, the plenum epistemologically, or the tempestuousness of the world personally.

The function of chaos: "old fogeyism"

Our sense of the chaotic has been strongly shaped by Milton and by the classical tradition he knew and used so thoroughly. In the cosmos of *Paradise Lost*, chaos is both a place, lying between heaven and hell, and the coruler of that abyss. It is

                              a dark
      Illimitable Ocean, without bound,
      Without dimension, where length, breadth, and highth,
      And time and place are lost; where eldest Night
      And Chaos, Ancestors of Nature, hold
      Eternal Anarchy, amidst the noise
      Of endless wars, and by confusion stand[92]

As with Ovid's "*rudis indigestaque moles*," or "rough,
unordered mass," it is a particularly utter disorder that is most
common, along with the effect of such disorder on humans:
tumult, confusion, and discord.[93] The world may be formed
from chaos, so in that sense chaos may have a part in creativity by being a source of potentiality, but preeminently chaos
is hostile and destructive. Satan himself would have perished
in the Abyss had not Chaos endorsed his aim of "havoc and
spoil and ruin."[94] It is that tradition that dominates our conception of chaos. It is one that James takes up in the midst of
his own havoc and ruin. It is also one that continues in the
Principles, in the "sorry plight" that would result were there
no habit, the worldly "blast" that tests our character, the
"weltering sea of sensibility and emotion" that rocks us from
within, the "immense sacrifice" that would result if we acted
mechanically, from reflex alone, and did not have a reservoir
of postponement and deliberation, and the "darkest confusion" of dysfunction that illumines the orderly flow of the
mind.

      Alongside of the hostile and destructive, we might
glimpse the germ of a productive sense of chaos in the traditional view. Milton sees the elements in perpetual strife.
"Unless th' Almighty Maker them ordain / His dark materials
to create more Worlds."[95] Ovid, too, says

            . . . discordant atoms warred . . .
            Til God, or kindlier Nature,
            Settled all argument, and separated
            Heaven from earth . . .
            So things evolved, and out of blind confusion
            Found each its place, bound in eternal order.[96]

The raw materials of the world exist in chaos, and the Demiurge need only fashion them into creation. It is possible for

the notion to arise that whatever excellence the world has may be traceable not only to God but to God's materials. Conversely, if the world is imperfect, it might be due to a lack of fidelity not only to its Maker but to its materials. Other possibilities exist, of course. We could blame the chaotic materials for imperfection or be grateful their strife is not more predominant. But we have to wonder where arises a notion like James's that the plenum holds a wealth from which we always fall short, or Henry Adams's that "chaos often breeds life, when order breeds habit." Without claiming too much, and certainly without going into a full history of the idea of chaos, some sense of the benefits of chaos does stand beside the more common destructive association with the chaotic. In any event, while such a notion may be taken up by James in his conception of the plenum, and while it may lie behind the general idea that chaos can be useful, it is different from James's sense of internal chaos.[97]

It is not construction that James sees going on in consciousness. The disordered is not fashioned into the ordered as Milton's atoms are composed into worlds. Rather, the chaotic is integral to mind (and body). Continuity and change are essential parts of consciousness along with the more limited and limiting aspects of personality and interest, which themselves are characterized by continuity and change. I have termed this integrated aspect *domesticated chaos*, one in which the relatively ordered and relatively disordered coexist and interact. We saw its first hints biographically where it was evident in James's ability to incorporate motion within limitation. We see it in each of the characteristics of consciousness, as each substantive or stable aspect is tied to a fluid and unstable one. We also see it in the neural stream.

Yet what is of importance in James's domesticated chaos is not what that chaos is but what it does. It is in its functioning that it is productive, and that it is integrated. As James will say in later works such as *Pragmatism*, what is important is the "cash-value" of a description such as this one, not its "truth." And what the chaotic does, in sum, might be described as combating rigidity or, in a favorite expression of James's, "old fogeyism."

The term arises in his discussion of perception where he states that "most of us grow more and more enslaved to the stock conceptions with which we have once become familiar, and less and less capable of assimilating impressions in any but the old ways."[98] Old fogeyism is the tyranny of the established. It exists not only in perception but in every aspect of mind that James explores. The presumption that our sensations are always the same, that "the same piano-key, struck with the same force, make[s] us hear in the same way," is one brand.[99] So is the notion that a thought refers to one thing only and not the "thousand other things" it also knows dimly in its fringe.[100] We might see another example in James's view of the merely mechanical in nature, that which does not display mind or intelligence but mechanically follows from the past.[101] Intelligence, humanity, and life are not so predictable or regular. This last is a departure from the others since it deals not with the mind but all of nature, but I would want to extend old fogeyism to such examples for they are pervasive in the *Principles* and seem to be important to James.

What they all have in common is rigidity and narrowness. In *Talks to Teachers* he discusses their effects: they chop up "the flowing life of the mind," neglect the full richness of experience, and inadequately handle our problems and dilemmas.[102] Such rigidity deadens; it produces a "deadness of spirits" perhaps similar to that experienced by James in his paralyzed crisis years. So in combating rigidity the chaotic also functions to allow fullness and richness to emerge, and to enable one to deal with the new. Not dominated by already existing structures, the mind is able to operate more subtly and more adequately. It is typical of James that in *Talks* he recommends a multiplicity of conceptual and perceptual categories to combat old fogeyism, but, in fact, the *Principles* (and *Talks*, as well) is quite centrally concerned with those aspects of consciousness that continuously and integrally struggle against rigidity. I might add that the chaotic has a much larger—a religious—function, as well. It operates to orient us in the largest dimensions of who we are, where we are, and where we are going. That is an issue, however, for the final chapter of this book.

So this is what the chaotic in James does: it combats rigidity in perception, sensation, consciousness, the sense of self, reasoning, willing, and all the other aspects of mind that James treats. At the same time it allows greater inclusiveness in all such operations. It widens our sensing, thinking, and acting beyond whatever limits may exist. The chaotic appears, then, as the juxtaposition of the unformed to the formed, the disordered to the ordered, or the unstructured to the structured, and it constantly challenges the more ordered forms to change. That is why the term, the *chaotic*, is so useful in dealing with James. It describes what aspects of mind such as continuity, change, the fringe, vagueness, and others *do* more adequately than a term like *fluidity* might. Moreover, the chaotic gathers in James's personal experience, his view of the plenum, and his idea of the neural stream that constitute a complex of ideas that flows through James's life and work at least until the early 1890s. In sum, if "mere mechanical sprouting" exemplifies what lacks mind and intelligence, we might say that humanity has intelligence and its distinctive liveliness in considerable part because of its domesticated chaos.

This has been quite a long and involved articulation of James's "chaotic" worldview. It is not, however, the whole story. Michael Riffaterre claims that we shouldn't make assumptions about the commonalities of different books by the same author. "The largest analyzable corpus that we conceive in literature should be the text and not a collection of texts."[103] We can't assume, then, that the view of chaos that we find in the *Principles* informs any of James's other books. I don't generally agree with Riffaterre, but following his advice can lead to interesting results. In the following chapter I shall look at *The Varieties of Religious Experience* somewhat independently, and present the view of chaos we may discover in its pages. Once we have gained a clear understanding of the worldview implicit in both books, we will turn to the second task of this study: an analysis of the role of the styles of these books in inculcating in readers the sense that the universe (and humans) are indeed "chaotic." Those later, stylistic chapters, then, will depend upon these earlier ones.

3
"The Floods and Waterspouts of God": The Chaotic in *The Varieties of Religious Experience*

Introduction

Shortly before James began planning the Gifford Lectures, which would become *The Varieties of Religious Experience*, he added a lecture to his "Talks to Students" series that he delivered quite frequently during the 1890s, as a companion to "Talks to Teachers." In that lecture, entitled, "What Makes a Life Significant," he describes the great distaste that a week's stay at Chautauqua prompted.[1] He calls the festival a "middle-class paradise, without a sin, without a victim, without a tear."[2] It is "a foretaste of what human society might be, were it all in the light, with no suffering and no dark corners." It seems significant that the celebration of health, happiness, intelligence, and creativity should cause such a reaction in James. He reports that when he left this is how he felt:

> Ouf! What a relief! Now for something primordial and savage, even though it were as bad as an Armenian massacre, to set the balance straight again. This order is too tame, this culture too second-rate, this goodness too uninspiring. This human drama without a villain or a pang; this community so refined that ice-cream soda-water is the utmost offering it can make to the brute animal in man; this city simmering in the tepid lakeside sun; this atrocious harmlessness of all things—I cannot abide with them. Let me take my chances again in the big outside worldly wilderness with all its sins and sufferings.[3]

Perhaps this reaction against an "irremediable flatness" and toward "human nature *in extremis*" reflects one of James's periodic oscillations.[4] Perry speaks of "the frequency of the barometric and thermometric changes in [James's] temperamental weather."[5] Perhaps it signals a deeper climatic change

51

in James, for in taking up the *Varieties* after reading the *Principles of Psychology* it seems that we have moved from a predominant sympathy for the level and light to one for the "heights and depths, the precipices and the steep ideals, the gleams of the awful and the infinite."[6]

James disparaged the *Varieties* once it was finished, as he had the *Principles*. His first book he called "the enormous rat which . . . ten years' gestation has brought forth."[7] The second was "perfunctory work—scissors and paste as much as possible."[8] Both characterizations belie the significance the works had for James, intellectually and personally. Far more than a mere pastiche of others' accounts of their religious experiences, the *Varieties* was "my own last will and testament" to James. He called it "a task well-nigh impossible . . . but to attempt it is *my* religious act."[9] We must wonder if the deep significance that the *Varieties* held for James didn't have something to do with its attempt to handle "human nature *in extremis*" instead of human nature *in normalis*, as in the *Principles*.

From the point of view of the chaotic, the *Varieties* offers a striking contrast to the *Principles*, for its predominant use of the chaotic is not characterized by integration and domestication but by sharp disjunction. The chaos of the *Varieties* is that of "utter confusion and disorder," the threatening form of formlessness that was so powerful a tool for Pascal, Hobbes, Shakespeare, and others, rather than the softened, even beneficial liberator of Henry Adams, Wallace Stevens, and Kate Chopin. It is somewhat surprising that the *Principles* did not deal with psychic pain considering James's own history and the work soon to be done by Freud; the *Varieties* fulfills whatever expectations in that direction we might have. If the *Principles* is a celebration of health, the *Varieties*, while certainly not extolling illness and pain, places it at the center of the fullest life. James's use of the chaotic accords with that change.

Biographical context

As the *Principles* was in a sense born out of James's years of crisis, the *Varieties* issued from the second significant period of ill-health in James's life, one that would end in his death eight years after the completion of the Gifford Lectures. The central event in the decline of James's health is generally taken to be a two-day climb of Mt. Marcy and other peaks in the Adirondacks in July 1898. "It was the steepest sort of work, and, as one looked from the summits, seemed sheer impossible," wrote the fifty-six-year-old climber himself days afterward.[10] As his son, Henry, notes, James had gone to the Adirondacks extremely fatigued and having suffered from insomnia. The strenuous climbing strained his heart, a condition that would plague him for the next twelve years and eventually claim his life in 1910.[11]

In general, 1898 was a physically and emotionally difficult year for James. Gay Wilson Allen comments that the year began with "sleeplessness and consequent nervous exhaustion."[12] Then came a crisis concerning James's brother, Robertson, who had long had a drinking problem and marital conflicts. After a particularly dissolute episode in Boston, he agreed to enter a sanitarium, and it fell to William to look after the matter. James's public involvements also resulted in a considerable amount of strain. In March he testified at a legislative hearing in opposition to a bill to require the licensing of all medical practitioners. His concern was for "mind-curers" whose success James could not fully understand, but whom he did not want to see excluded from their efforts. His speech aroused the active enmity of much of the Boston medical community. "I never did anything that required as much moral effort in my life," he wrote afterward.[13] James's public criticism of American imperialism during the Spanish-American War, which was declared in April of that year, also required considerable moral effort and, no doubt, added to the strain on him. Charles Eliot Norton's resignation from the Harvard faculty was demanded and submitted after he criticized the war in particularly strong terms, and James, too, was under pressure to desist in his public stance.[14] On the heels of these stressful involvements and his usual exhaustion at the end of the school term came the Mt. Marcy climb. James's health never fully recovered.

In the shorter term, the period in which he was prepar-

ing the Gifford Lectures was characterized by invalidism,
numerous journeys for treatment, and considerable depression. The lectures that had originally been scheduled for Jan-
uary or February of 1900 were postponed several times, as
James found himself unable to work. They were finally delivered in May 1901. Early in 1900 James wrote Henry William
Rankin, "I can hardly read anything and cannot write at all."[15]
Late in that same year he wrote Charles W. Eliot, "After a fort-
night of work two hours a day, I have to knock off for a
month."[16] As in the earlier crisis, James moved restlessly
about Europe, seeking physical and emotional relief. This
time it was the spa at Nauheim instead of Teplitz, but the
results were just as equivocal and may have actually been
harmful. When he wasn't taking the cure, he was staying
with Henry either in London or Rye; trying the baths in
Malvern; recuperating in Provence; or making stops in
Geneva, Heidelberg, Rome, Paris, or Lucerne. James himself
described his mental state as "irritability and fits of despair
and invalid egotism."[17] In spite of the nearly constant company of his wife, and the occasional companionship of
Henry, his daughter Peggy, and many other friends and
admirers, what was foremost to James was that "I am left to
suffer alone, alone, alone."[18] In all it was, in James's characteristically vivid words, "two years of the dull twilight of vegetative existence."[19]

The period shared with the crisis years physical disability,
frequent inability to use his eyes, insomnia, enforced rest,
and the inability to work productively, along with a resulting
dejection natural in a man so vitally energetic. But what is
striking about the similarity between the two periods is that
such different books resulted, for the *Principles* surely presents the healthy mind while the *Varieties* speaks from the
sick soul. Possibly the greater severity of the earlier condition
made normalcy and health paramount concerns. Then
James's ill-health at the end of the century put him in mind
once again of the seriousness of pain and evil, and by then he
had achieved sufficient maturity and stability that his writing
could now address such suffering, rather than attempt to
cure it.

There is an indication of this change in James's remarks about nature during these two "twilight" years. As we saw in the earlier period, the way in which James imagined his situation indicated his longing to transform the destructive tumult of the world into an internalized and domesticated motion. During the two invalid years in Europe before the Gifford Lectures, his imagination frequently turns to nature, particularly to the contrast between nature in Europe and America. Soon after arriving in Europe in 1899, James complains about the German weather for being "stagnant and immovable. It is as if it got stuck, and needed a kick to start it."[20] The yearning for motion superficially seems similar to the travels of the 1860s, but the character of the desired motion is quite different. James sees European nature as a landscape, that is, as humanly shaped land. It is "fenced or planted" or "too padded and cushioned."[21] What he wants instead of European stagnation is "our glorious quick passionate American climate." "I crave some wild American country," he writes soon before he returns in 1901.[22] There is no indication in these statements that James seeks to incorporate the motion that American wilderness offers. There is nothing domesticated about the "wild" that he seeks.

In fact, his image of American nature seems to recall the "Walpurgis Nacht" James describes at the time of his fateful climb of Mt. Marcy in 1898. In a "wakeful mood," he slept little the night before the climb, spending it watching the moonlight, sky, and woods, and "got into a state of spiritual alertness of the most vital description." I should quote his account at length.

> It became a regular Walpurgis Nacht. I spent a good deal of it in the woods, where the streaming moonlight lit up things in a magical checkered play, and it seemed as if the Gods of all the nature-mythologies were holding an indescribable meeting in my breast with the moral Gods of the inner life. The two kinds of Gods have nothing in common—the Edinburgh [Gifford] lectures made quite a hitch ahead. The intense significance of some sort, of the whole scene, if one could only *tell* the significance; the intense inhuman remoteness of its inner life, and yet the intense *appeal* of it; its everlasting freshness and its

immemorial antiquity and decay . . . [were] part and parcel of it all, and beaten up with it."[23]

The account offers quite an insight into what nature represents to James in this period. Nature is not planted or fenced, not a garden or a field; rather it is the place of the witches' sabbath. In Goethe's account,

> Branches moaning and breaking!
> Tree-trunks mightily thundering!
> Roots creaking and yawning!
> Tree upon tree in appalling
> Confusion crashing and falling,
> And through the wreckage on the scarps
> The winds are hissing and howling.[24]

While James is not witnessing the literal upheaval that Goethe depicts, his "state of spiritual alertness" involves an upheaval, nonetheless. Nature is inhuman; it is remote. James's experience seems to be an epiphany of the chaotic. Nature issues a challenge to orderliness, and it does so by being fresh, ancient, and decaying; that is, it breaks with all that is accustomed and intact. Moreover, this alternative force reaches back to the remote origins—we might even say to primordial times of *rudis indigestaque moles*. It really does seem as though what appeals to James about nature is its wildness.

James's sense of the wild in nature stands outside that predominant in America in the late nineteenth century. While John Muir preaches that "nature's peace will flow into you as the sunshine into the trees. The winds will blow their freshness into you, and the storms their energy, while cares drop off like autumn leaves,"[25] James's view is more equivocal. Along with freshness is decay, and the energy of the wild is as disturbing as it is invigorating. While the end of the century looked to nature to repair morality,[26] James perceives that the nature gods have nothing in common with the moral gods of the inner life. This is not cause to flee, as it might have been in an earlier America, or cause to feel threatened with extinction, as it might have been in an earlier William James. At the end of the century James acutely feels the greatly disruptive aspects of a "lost, unruly, disordered, or confused" nature and to consider that they constitute an experience that is both vital and spiritual.

The chaotic in *The Varieties of Religious Experience*

The *Principles of Psychology* describes an external world that is a roiling caldron of elements from which interest creates an order. I compared that plenum to the Timaean kaos from which the demiurge self fashions the world; it becomes the ideal of inclusiveness to which consciousness aspires. If anything exists "at base" in the *Varieties*, it is not potentiality but evil. Evil can be ignored or it can be faced, but it never disappears. Unlike the plenum, it is something that no one desires; like it, evil demands to be taken into account.

When it comes to James's discussion of evil—of death, illness, and suffering—his prose is vivid but the evil seems less than terrifying.

> Here on our very hearths and in our gardens the infernal cat plays with the panting mouse, or holds the hot bird fluttering in her jaws. Crocodiles and rattlesnakes and pythons are at this moment vessels of life as real as we are; their loathsome existence fills every minute of every day that drags its length along.[27]

Such evil does not sound especially radical; it reminds me of the "Victorian pessimism" that Stanley Kauffmann saw in Matthew Arnold: it seems to suggest that there is a comforting cup of tea waiting somewhere in the cosmic void.[28] Natural evil does not really seem to be James's concern. After all, his reaction to the great San Francisco earthquake of 1906 was "admiration for the way a wooden house could prove its elasticity, and glee over the vividness of the manner in which such an 'abstract idea' as 'earthquake' could verify itself into sensible reality."[29] Appropriately enough, it is James's discussion of how evil functions in peoples' lives that strikes us as strong, full, and apt. And, in a word, evil functions chaotically.

The problem with evil is not pain and suffering but insecurity. There is no order; rather evil and good seem merely
thrown together in a disordered mixture. "To begin with,"
James states, "how *can* things so insecure as the successful
experiences of this world afford a stable anchorage? . . . In
the healthiest and most prosperous existence, how many
links of illness, danger, and disaster are always interposed?"
James's answer is not that there are too many links of evil,
but that there is an unknown number, in an unknown
sequence. We never know when failure and death will arise.
We are left with "an irremediable sense of precariousness."
Blessedness is a "fragile fiction." We "strew" our lives with
blunders. In short, good and evil are unbearably random: "life
and its negation are beaten up inextricably together."[30]

The result, and a chief characteristic of the sick soul, is
confusion. It is distinguished from despair and meaninglessness as chaos is distinguished from evil. The sick soul doesn't
feel that all is ill; rather he or she is uncertain just what the
state of the world is. Perplexity is the result. Whatever we
have, whatever sense we've made of the world, is sure to be
swept away, leaving us in disarray.

In speaking of Tolstoy, James presents a fascinating
account of perplexity that picks up several of the topics of
the *Principles*. James explains that values are not dependent
on facts. That is, the same facts may be perceived to have
widely different emotional value. "Whatever of value, interest, or meaning our respective worlds may appear endued
with are thus pure gifts of the spectator's mind."[31] As James
said in the *Principles*, reality is actually a plenum and our
interest alone divides it into what has meaning for us.[32] In
Tolstoy's case, James says, perplexity arose because "the
excitement and interest which our functions naturally bring
had ceased."[33] Without interest, the world is only the
plenum, lacking value or meaning. This is quite a different
account than James had given earlier. Previously evil was a
basic fact—"the evil background is really there to be thought
of";[34] now, all is created, and the problem arises when we
create nothing at all. It's the usual difficulty with James's vac-
illation concerning just how strong a role humans take in

forming themselves and their worlds. My task isn't to reconcile the two, but to show how strongly the chaotic figures in both accounts. According to the first, at any moment evil can arise and shake the stability of our lives. According to the second, since we are without the creative activity of interest, any meaning or value that we have is swept away by the randomness of the sheer plenum. In both cases, chaos comes from the destruction of an orderly sense of self and world. "Things [are] meaningless whose meaning had always been self-evident."[35] Perplexity is a characteristic of both accounts and the sick soul is in a chaotic state of utter disorder and confusion.

James's treatment of the sick soul is not the only place where chaos figures. One who is unable simply to write evil off and live happily as the healthy-minded can is condemned, says James, to have a divided self. It is somewhat difficult to see exactly what the relationship is between the sick soul and the divided self. James seems to be saying that the challenge of evil is so great that we come into conflict with ourselves. The attempt to integrate evil is enormously difficult, and we characteristically take two approaches, which James labels "the natural and the spiritual," "the higher and the lower," "the useful and the erring," and "the actual and the ideal."[36] A number of points should be made: first, James terms it a division into selves to indicate the scope of the process. The creation of a complete self is involved, as is the creation of a world.[37] The outcome of the struggle determines who we are and what the world is, which is to say, it has great pragmatic consequences. Second, there are *two* selves. The stream of selves that he wrote of in the *Principles* is gone. There is no continuity, no fluidity here: there are two and they are "deadly hostile" to one another.[38] Third, the two selves are qualitatively different. One is better and one worse. They seem to be divided on how well they function: the "higher" is better able to integrate all that must be taken account of. The "lower" has less perspective. Fourth and finally, the two selves create chaos. In contrast to the stream of selves that generally coexisted so smoothly, "the higher and the lower feelings, the useful and erring impulses, begin by being a comparative chaos within." The discrepancy between selves "makes havoc of the subject's life. "In an instance of the sort of form that the chaotic can take, James describes such an existence as "little more than a series of zig zags." Religion becomes a search for order, a point I will discuss in more detail later. All I wish to point out now is that James sees religion as a way of "reaching unity": "firmness, stability, and equilibrium [succeed] a period of storm and stress and inconsistency."[39] So while the encounter of the sick soul with evil creates a chaos of perplexity by undermining the habitual manner of making sense of the world,[40] the process of coming to terms with evil is chaotic, as well, since competing integrating views, which is to say competing selves, create disorder.

The manner in which the chaotic operates in the sick soul and divided self contrasts quite strongly with its operation in the *Principles*. We have defined the chaotic very loosely in terms of contrast, that there is a relative disorder that challenges the more stable and orderly. The prevalent pattern in the *Principles* was of a chaos that was not disruptive; the chaotic was integral to mind. It functioned to combat rigidity by dissolving it in multiplicity, continuity, indeterminacy, and change. All take place in a very fluid fashion. In the *Principles*, as we said, the chaotic is domesticated. The *Varieties* presents a very different view. People are thrown into chaos by the evil of the world or by their inability to sort the world into a meaningful order. Such chaos is dangerous, creating anguish, by undermining the stabilities that support life. There is nothing domesticated or integrated about such chaos. It is abrupt and wrenching. And even when "firmness, stability, and equilibrium" are achieved, when conversion takes place and the "higher self" is realized—that is, when order replaces chaos—it takes place as an annihilation of the old by the new.

The divided self is eventually unified in conversion. From chaos comes order, and instrumental in that change is the subconscious. James's theory of the subliminal self is certainly one of his most striking and important. Building, he says, on work done by others, but in fact in a direction all his own, James suggests the existence of two selves, one conscious and one beyond the ordinary margins of consciousness.[41] What takes place in conversion is a sudden incursion from the subliminal self so that the conscious self is changed: the "field of consciousness" is now larger, and, accordingly its "habitual centre" shifts. We are new persons; we are born anew. Though James says that conversions can be either voluntary or involuntary, gradual or abrupt, it is the sudden that he takes as more basic.[42] In such a transformation the subliminal self *bursts* into consciousness, *rupturing* not only the margin of consciousness but the old self, as well. In speaking of the process, James sometimes uses imagery of gradual transformation, describing the self as frozen and in need of a thaw.[43] He declares that "something must give way, a native hardness must break down and liquefy."[44] More commonly he uses liquid imagery that contrasts more strongly with the metaphors of the flowing stream or bountiful reservoir that were so prevalent in the *Principles*. He states that one way in which "anger, worry, fear, despair" or other emotions of the sick soul can be banished is if "an opposite affection should overpoweringly break over us."[45] The type is given explicitly when he concludes the chapter on conversion by saying that "the higher condition, having reached the due degree of energy, bursts through all barriers and sweeps in like a sudden flood."[46]

It is common enough—as any newspaper account will attest—to describe the result of a burst dam as chaos. It is somewhat instructive to see why. It is not violence that is the touchstone of chaos but disorder, and disorder is relative. Rushing waters are not inherently chaotic. A white water kayaker sees no chaos in crosscurrents, channels, souse holes, and chutes. Being no kayaker, I see chaos, but what does that mean? The kayaker sees order, whereas I find an absence of order. Rushing waters are only disorderly in contrast with order. Such contrast can come about in a number of ways. The torrent could have come about from the destruction of a dam in which case a viewer could see them as chaotic in contrast to their own prior stability. They could be chaotic because of the disorder they cause, as in buildings

splintered and cars tossed about. In this case, we must contrast splinters and upended vehicles with their more normal,
orderly condition. Or, regardless of a burst dam, the rushing
waters could be seen as chaotic in contrast to a conceived
orderliness, as when we watch the swirls of a rapids and
compare it to the more linear motion of a more gentle river.
Take away the contrast and you take away the chaos.

The chaos that exists in the *Varieties* is similar to that in
the *Principles* by its dependence on contrast. In the case of
conversion, extramarginal material bursts through the margin
of consciousness and floods the field of consciousness. From
the point of view of the self whose margins are burst, the
flood is sheer chaos in contrast with its prior—relative—order.
Its buildings and cars—its concepts and understandings—are
shattered and tossed, and it remembers their prior stability.
The difference between chaos in the two books is in both
the degree of violence in the contrast and in the attitude
toward the disorder. The extramarginal material *bursts* while
the stream of selves *dissolves* the boundaries of the self. In
both cases there is relative disorder; the first is the chaos of
Othello, *Leviathan*, and *Paradise Lost*, and the second that
of "Sunday Morning," *The Awakening*, and *The Education
of Henry Adams*.[47] In addition, and perhaps as a consequence, the violent chaos tends to be more threatening and
the gentle chaos to be seen as beneficial.

The total picture of religious crisis (or of any extreme
change in personality)[48] is one in which the chaotic plays an
integral role. For the sick soul, evil is mixed randomly with
good, creating confusion as habitual ways of making sense of
the self and world are undermined. The self is divided in the
attempt to come to terms with evil, making a "battleground"
of the inner world. Finally, a subconscious integration forms
and bursts through the boundaries of consciousness throw-
ing the old self into chaos momentarily but creating at last a
degree of "firmness, stability, and equilibrium."

It seems to be an unusual side of James to long for and
value order, particularly considering his preference for the
vague, the indeterminate, and the fluid in the *Principles*. Yet
that seems precisely the case in the *Varieties*. Domesticated

chaos functioned well in the *Principles*' study of the healthy mind: it combated rigidity and enabled the mind to be inclusive. But in much of the *Varieties* it is storm and stress that is the problem; accordingly, James conceives order as having greater usefulness.

Religion is a way of "reaching unity": the "comparative chaos" of the higher and lower selves "must end by forming a stable system of functions in right subordination." In Tolstoy's case, "his crisis was the getting of his soul in order. . . . It was a case of heterogeneous personality tardily and slowly finding its unity and level."[49] The story of Augustine, Bunyan, David Brainerd, Stephen Bradley, and all the others James cites, famous and obscure, is one of intolerable chaos being transformed into order.

James conceives saintliness in terms of the order that it provides and the discord that it holds in check. The central characteristic of the "state of assurance" that the converted possess is peace, harmony, and loss of worry.[50] Such calm comes from the sense that all is related to the "divine order."[51] It is a common phrase, and it is easy to overlook the particular emphasis that James places on it. The saint passes from personal chaos to divine order, and that order is an important aspect of the value of saintliness. Similarly, God is conceived of as "the guarantee of an ideal order that shall be permanently preserved . . . where God is, tragedy is only provisional and partial, and shipwreck and dissolution [and, we might add, chaos] are not the absolutely final things."[52]

Saintliness, of course, is not a finished state, and the continual strivings of the saint also have to do with order and disorder. The saintly person "becomes exceedingly sensitive to inner inconsistency or discord, and mixture and confusion grow intolerable."[53] A frequent consequence is the withdrawal to monasteries in search of "changeless order" where "the holy-minded person finds that inner smoothness and cleanness which it is torture to him to feel violated at every turn by the discordancy and brutality of secular existence."[54]

James's shift from sympathy for such searches for harmony to disapproval is subtle. It is unmistakable in his criticism of the saintly virtue of purity. Some, he says, require a simplified, orderly world.

> Variety and confusion are too much for their powers of comfortable adaptation. But whereas your aggressive pietist reaches his unity objectively, by forcibly stamping disorder and divergence out, your retiring pietist reaches his subjectively, leaving disorder in the world at large, but making a smaller world in which he dwells himself and from which he eliminates it altogether.[55]

James seems to have little admiration or sympathy for those choosing comfort over variety, and unity over divergence or breadth. The religious recluse dwells in an airless cell. It is the Jamesian virtue of inclusiveness that is violated in the excesses of saintliness; it is that virtue, too, that makes the threat of the chaotic somewhat more equivocal than it seemed in James's discussion of the sick soul, divided self, and conversion. Divine order may offer respite from a wrenching, chaotic perplexity, but a restrictive obsession with order is no answer.

As far back as 1869 James wondered if the mind could be "so purely fluid and plastic" that it could "sympathize with the total process of the universe."[56] It's a value he never lost. In the *Principles* the desire for inclusiveness seems to fuel much of what I've termed *domesticated chaos*. "All narrow people *intrench* their Me, they retract it,—from the region of what they cannot securely possess," he states. Whereas "all sympathetic people . . . proceed by the entirely opposite way of expansion and inclusion. The outline of their self often gets uncertain enough, but for this the spread of its content more than atones."[57] So the stream of selves includes more than a well-defined and limited self would, even if it results in indistinctness and instability. Similarly, attention, conception, and reasoning function best when the active power of the mind, interest, moves most broadly, taking in as much of the full wealth of the world as possible.[58]

The desire for inclusiveness, in sum, is one strong reason for James's commitment to variety and pluralism. That affinity for variety is too pervasive in his writing to need demonstration. A fine figure for it is his description of his house in the Adirondacks. "Oh, it's the most delightful house you ever saw; it has 14 doors, all opening outwards."[59] The only thing better than fourteen doors for James would be fourteen more, and in the *Varieties* he presents at least that many through which men and women have passed in the religious life.

The *Varieties* contains the same passion for inclusiveness and variety. The universe is a "many-sided affair" so it's natural that individuals exhibit "enormous diversity" in their spiritual lives, and that "the world can be handled according to many systems of ideas."[60] But the only way to do justice to such diversity is constantly to attempt to be more inclusive. "There never can be a state of facts to which new meaning may not truthfully be added, provided the mind ascend to a more enveloping point of view."[61] And, at least in this work, James feels that such expansion results in perplexity.[62] Current views, like current selves, must be burst for new views, larger views to take their place. Cohesion, unity, and order cannot be too highly valued for then we would not attempt to open more doors. Perplexity, disorder—chaos in our understanding and in our lives—not only must be endured if we value diversity and inclusiveness, they are the *sine qua non* of moving toward them.

James seems to see a similar choice when he considers theory and experience. In planning the Gifford Lectures, he wrote a friend that he sought to deal with religious experience, "patently absurd" as most of its manifestations seem to be.[63] Yet James seems not really to mind that absurdness; in fact, it may constitute part of the appeal of religion for him. The absurd, from the Latin, *absurdus*, is literally the deaf, the voiceless, and hence the irrational. James takes particular pains in the *Varieties* to distinguish living religion from systems of ideas, what he terms "overbeliefs." In comparison with dogma, religious experience is voiceless and irrational, and that is in its favor. "Warranted systems," he says, "have ever been the idols of aspiring souls. All-inclusive, yet simple; noble, clean, luminous, stable, rigorous, true;—what more ideal refuge could there be than such a system would offer to spirits vexed by the muddiness and accidentality of the world of sensible things."[64] The devotees of overbelief seem much like the anchorites he criticizes in his discussion of saintliness. Systematic thought offers a refuge of order and stability in a disorderly world. In contrast James prefers the instability, incompleteness, and vagueness of the experiential. "As soon as we deal with private and personal phenomena as such, we deal with realities in the completest sense of the term."[65]

It is revealing that James takes religious experience to be in conflict with the philosophical or systematic expression of it. "Whenever a procedure is codified, the more delicate spirit of it evaporates," he states.[66] And that, in general, is his point of view. Genuine religion is challenging. "A genuine first-hand religious experience . . . is bound to be a heterodoxy to its witnesses." And if it catches on to become orthodoxy it "can be henceforth counted on as a staunch ally in every attempt to stifle the spontaneous religious spirit, and to stop all later bubbling fountains."[67] Religious experience is as subversive to orthodoxy for James as it is for his father's friend, Emerson. He compares the truly religious to anarchists and socialists. "They help to break the edge of the general reign of hardness."[68]

In brief, the absurdity of religious experience functions chaotically with respect to dogma, system, and philosophy. It does not respect their definitions and clarifications. It is anarchic, heretical, heterodox. It bursts the bounds of theological formulations, creating perplexity for those who are committed to the orthodox orders, but creating, too, the possibility of new ways of being and understanding.

Religion and the chaotic

James states that the critic can aspire to impartiality, but he or she must also be a participant, "and he is sure to approve most warmly those fruits of piety in others which taste most good and prove most nourishing to him."[69] What we want to know, what the *Varieties* itself compels us to ask, is: Where does James stand? What tastes good and is nourishing to him? It seems clear that James's judgment on those forms of saintliness and philosophy, which flee disorder and divergence, is negative, while his sympathy for the plight of those ravaged by the chaotic encounter with evil is profound. That which functions chaotically, be it evil, the divided self, conversion, inclusiveness, or religious experience, can be useful or not; it can be destructive or productive. In the end, James is not judging the chaotic, either implicitly or explicitly. It is not a term that frequently appears in his writing, as I've mentioned. It certainly is an idea that proliferates in his thought, but even as such, James's judgments are not based on it, however terrible the disorder in his own life and the lives of those he writes about.

Yet James's judgment about the truth and value of religion is put very much in terms of considerations that I have been calling chaotic. In his conclusion to the *Varieties* he contrasts the scientific view with the religious. The view given by science, he says, is of our planet and its life as a "local accident in an appalling wilderness of worlds." On the largest and smallest scales, the universe is merely "the drifting of the cosmic atoms." Reality is "aimless weather," in a typically pungent phrase.[70] It is certainly an image of mere chaos that this depiction conjures up, much like the "infinite chaos of movements, of which physics teaches us that the outer world consists," or the "irremediable flux . . . mere mechanical sprouting from the past, occurring with no reference to the future," both mentioned in the *Principles*.[71]

It is revealing that James does not characterize the religious life, then, as oriented toward order and purpose. He does say that "God's existence is the guarantee of an ideal order," but he also states that God is not the purpose of religion.[72] Expansion, inclusion are the aims and benefits of religion. "Not God but life, more life, a larger, richer, more satisfying life, is in the last analysis the end of religion."[73] The religious feelings are "of the cheerful, expansive, 'dynamogenic' order which, like any tonic, freshens our vital powers."[74] Through religion one gets in touch with a "more," and that is a notion quite congenial to James. It throws open one more door through which life can be larger and richer. James is quite aware that the expansiveness does not take in only beauty and love, for in major part the lectures and book have presented evil and anguish. James's concluding judgment of religion reinforces his decision against healthy-mindedness, against its harmony and calm in shutting out melancholy and despair. He is willing to sacrifice complete religious consolation and admit "the possibility of there being portions of the universe that may irretrievably be lost."[75] The religious perspective, then, like that of the materialist, is formed in view of the chaotic. Melancholy, perplexity, and despair are still possible. Evil—its implication that the world is a mere mixture, and its consequence that we become depressed and confused—evil still exists. The perplexing consequences of the commitment to variety and pluralism still exist. The religious view, in brief, both tolerates and creates the chaotic. The difference between the scientific and the religious is not so much their conception of chaos. The world to the melancholic—to James himself in the French correspondent passage—is much like "aimless weather." There is utter disorder and confusion in both. What is different is the vital energy that religion gives that allows it to be so inclusive. Following Tolstoy, James calls it *that by which men live*." He terms it "a stimulus, an excitement, a faith, a force that re-infuses the positive willingness to live, even in full presence of the evil perceptions that erewhile made life seem unbearable."[76]

4
"Meanderings, Zigzags, and Circles": Creating Chaos in *The Principles of Psychology*

Introduction

Sigmund Freud and his biographer, Ernest Jones, take an occasional look at William James, and together they find three matters particularly worth mentioning. The first is an admiration of James's apparently fearless attitude toward death, the second is the psychoanalyst's estimation of James's pragmatism as "anarchy," and the last is Jones's comment on the American's style of writing. Henry James, notes Jones, wrote novels like textbooks and William wrote textbooks like novels.[1] All three comments seem apt considering psychoanalysis' estimation of the motive power of the fear of death, its concern with combating disorder, and its ambiguous relationship to style: its concern to be scientific and hence understated and flat, and yet its dependence on the narration of case histories.

But focusing on these three—on man, philosophy, and manner of writing—is also somewhat surprising, for while we might well pair the first two, especially in a biography, we wouldn't ordinarily add the last, the concern with style, except in a literary analysis. Its inclusion demonstrates Jones's acuteness, for he realizes that manner of writing is close to the core in James. And that does not just mean that style is important to him; it means that were we to choose three aspects of James to depict him most effectively, they would be the man, the philosophy, and the manner, who he was, what he said, and how he said it. The last is usually considered to be ancillary, *merely* a matter of style, worthy of emphasis only when threatening to propel itself out of balance in a figure like Nietzsche. Yet with James, as with anyone, I would claim, neglecting the manner of his writing can lead to as deprived a depiction as neglecting the person or the thought. The manner does not simply add; it is not a bonus, a candy coating to help the medicine go down. It is essential. In fact, for any writer there is never an absence of manner. There is always some manner or other, and, moreover, it is integral to what is being said or who is saying it. Another manner of writing means another matter and means another man or woman, too.

The study of style or form has long been central in literary disciplines, but less attention has been paid to it in such areas as philosophy and theology. There the thought seems so preeminently important that the manner of writing becomes merely facilitative, and one either has a bad style that obscures or a good style that is clear. The manner is simply a pane of glass that a thinker can or cannot keep clean. Occasionally someone comes along whose style intrudes so strongly—Nietzsche, Rousseau, or Kierkegaard—that it challenges the ideal of transparency.[2] But manner is never negligible, even in Karl Barth or Kant.

What is involved, of course, is the form-content dichotomy, which has long been declared misleading, but that persists nonetheless. And what needs closer examination are the implications of form for content, that is, we need to look at what is successfully *said* by such formal aspects as style or genre. Narrative is one form that has received considerable attention over the past several years. I'd like to begin by presenting some of that before returning to man, matter, and manner in James.

The constructive role of form

Genre realism

I would like to argue that the form of a work has a strong influence on the way in which readers view themselves and the world. In other words, form constructs; it is an element in worldmaking, to use Nelson Goodman's terms.[3] This position is opposed to those who take a realist view of the mimetic function of form. That is to say, those who feel that narrative (or any other form) is merely a natural reflection of the way "things are" tend to treat form as inevitable and invariable. Consequently, there seems to be more talk about what a genre is than what it does; about the truthfulness of narrative rather than its appropriateness; more about its accuracy than about its function. The belief that reality does not mandate one particular form opens up options to scrutiny, and the consequence of form rather than its truth becomes paramount.

Stephen Crites represents the realist position particularly clearly and eloquently. Forms of cultural expression, he says, are not accidental. "They are not products of culture, much less products of individual choice and contrivance."[4] Narrative is an invariable because it is the form of experience itself. Crites comes to this conclusion by an analysis of memory and anticipation. Memory is "elemental" and "fixed" in its "simple order of succession.[11] Anticipation takes place by framing little stories about how things may fall out." The present embraces memory and anticipation "within a richer narrative form." Since our experience is narrative, then, only literary narrative can fully do justice to it. "Only narrative time can contain the tensions, surprises, disappointments, and reversals and achievements of actual, temporal experience."[5] Narrative is not one genre among others, it is the preeminent genre since it alone corresponds to actual experience.[6]

The question we need to direct at Crites is whether we can really know what the *actual* shape of our experience is. Can we authenticate a genre? And is one or another form valuable because it corresponds to the truth? That seems to be an error on both theoretical and practical grounds. Contemporary linguistic philosophers such as Hilary Putnam, Nelson Goodman, and Richard Rorty argue strongly that we can never leave behind cultural tools like language in order to examine experience and discover what its "elemental," "simple" nature is. We cannot just forget the cultural truism that time is successive, close our eyes, and examine our experience of time. Whatever we discover must be culturally shaped, so it's no great surprise that the conclusion is that actual experience is successive. On the practical side, there's no mechanism for resolution of disputes. Stephen Crites sees real experience as successive. Ted Estess replies that experience is really chaotic and that narrative is merely imposed upon it.[7] Aside from the theoretical problem remaining the same for Estess—how does he know existence is chaotic?—how do we decide who is correct, as we must if truth is our concern? We're left with competing raids on the inarticulate; left, too, with the dangers of dogmatism that can so easily result from such attempts.[8]

One consequence of the realist position is that experience is impoverished. Is memory only successive? Is our conception of the future strictly in the form of anticipatory stories? Surely we have numerous conceptions of memory and the future. They may be successive or they may be of discrete events, unconnected to what precedes or succeeds. Order may be reversed or completely jumbled, linked associatively if at all. We can simply never be passive recording devices— except in a particularly mechanistic model, which is itself, of course, another cultural shaping. All of our conceptions of memory or anticipation are *conceptions*, and if we restrict ourselves to one—our memory is only successive—we run the risk of making our experience a thinner affair than it otherwise would be. Another consequence is that we neglect what genres can *do*: they become mirrors of the world instead of shapers of it. I believe that it is critical to examine the consequences of form since they may contribute so strongly to who we are, where we are, and what we do.

The constructivist view of narrative

Though a realist view of genre is widespread, there is also a considerable body of opinion that opposes it, particularly among French critics. In the mid-1960s, Gerard Genette, Roland Barthes, and Tzvetan Todorov each articulated a view of the artificiality of narrative, a view that peels it away from faithful contiguity with reality and asserts its interpretive nature.

In one of the earlier statements, Genette disputes the

notion that there is nothing more natural than narrative. "The evolution of literature and of literary consciousness in the last half century will have had, among other fortunate consequences, that of drawing our attention . . . to the singular, artificial, and problematic aspect of the narrative act."[9] In the best spirit of criticism, Genette points out what seems obvious after he says it: that it is only direct speech that can be directly imitated; all else is represented. Quotation alone is "perfect imitation." It is the difference between reading "I raised my eyes and saw a boy running along the narrow, cracked path" and reading "In ten minutes it will be eight o'clock." The second is indistinguishable from the actual words spoken while the first is a presentation of events, not the events themselves. But Genette goes on to argue that perfect imitation is not imitation at all: that all imitation must involve representation.[10] The words on the page are not the words spoken: they are represented in print. Consequently, all that is possible in narrative is the "illusion of [perfect] mimesis."[11]

Borges makes a similar point in a short story of a man who makes a map that is exactly equal in size to the area that it represents. A map that perfectly imitates a place would perfectly correspond to that place: it would repeat it inch for inch. In fact, it would be that place. All representation, on the other hand, involves choices, selections, omissions. As Nelson Goodman writes, "Representing is a matter of classifying objects rather than of imitating them, of characterizing rather than of copying."[12] Narrative involves just such choices, selections, and omissions.[13]

Once the sanction of "reality," "life," or "experience" is removed from a genre, we are able to look at the consequences of each genre, at what each does. For my purposes, what each does is create its own world. As Todorov states, each genre has its own, internal verisimilitude to which we are bound while we are within it.[14] Barthes makes a similar point when he says that "the function of narrative is not to 'represent,' it is to *constitute* a spectacle still very enigmatic for us but in any case not of a mimetic order."[15] It is a striking phrase: a narrative (or any other genre) "constitutes a spectacle." The theatrical metaphor seems apt: genre puts on a show, and, as in good theater, that spectacle is our world while we view it.

What sort of world does narrative constitute? In general we might characterize narrative as a form composed of sequential events that are causally linked: that is, there is a plot. Narrative has coherence in thematic development, characterization, and imagery: that is, every part makes sense and contributes to the whole. Finally, there is a magisterial overview: the story is told by someone who has vision, knowledge, and voice. If the form constitutes the world for us, it persuades us that events are sequential and causally linked; that character is coherent, and objects, people, and ideas contribute to a unified meaning; and that we are (at least potentially) able to survey people and events and know where they are going and who or what they are. It is important to note that narrative form alone accomplishes this "world-making." *Any* narrative will tend to inculcate such a view in readers or listeners.[16]

It is also important to note that this is a selective construction of the world. As Alastair Fowler notes, "We must suppose that genres offer distinctive possibilities of vision, and distinctive limitations."[17] The narrator is largely external to events, privileged and encompassing in knowledge, authoritative in articulation, and public in proclamation. One dimension that is lacking in such a depiction and such a construction is that of limitation, partiality, personality, intimacy, and subjection to events and others. That is a world that cannot be created by narrative, one that has its own value, and for which we might look to lyric.

And yet another world for which we cannot look to narrative is that depicted in William James's works, the chaotic world. In fact, could there be a world for which narrative is more inappropriate? Sequentiality and causality; coherence in objects, people, and ideas; magisterial overview? There would need to be a great deal of tinkering with narrative form to constitute a chaotic spectacle.

What, then, is the form appropriate to constructing a chaotic world? The immediate inclination is to say no form at all or one that is itself chaotic, that is, unreadable. And the cynical among us might think of *Finnegans Wake* or Beckett's *Molloy*. Yet, considering what I've said about chaos, a formless mess would not be an apt form, first because a formless mess is impossible for humans to construct,[18] and second because chaos is not formless. So some particular literary form would constitute the form of the chaotic. I do not propose to solve this question abstractly, thank goodness; cooking up a theoretical chaotic genre. Rather, James has provided us with two texts that speak about chaotic worlds, and what I propose to do is to look at the manners in which those works are written to see if their forms make chaotic worlds. Moreover, since the kinds of chaos are so different, one domesticated, the other more disruptive, we might expect that their forms create different chaotic worlds, as well.

The form of *The Principles of Psychology*

James's "rhetoric"

William James was a man as interested in the manner of communication as in the ideas to be communicated, so it is not surprising that shortly after the publication of the *Principles* he began delivering the lecture series, *Talks to Teachers*. The lectures represent James's own exercise in manners of communication, an attempt to use a different form than the written text to speak of psychology. They also directly concern the importance of manner in communication, for though they are designed to acquaint teachers with the minds of their pupils, they are also lectures on pedagogy: James uses his knowledge of human psychology to suggest the most useful techniques in teaching. At the same time the lectures concern rhetoric, for the techniques that he presents are useful not only for engaging students' interest and attention, but those of readers, as well. In fact, many of his discussions seem to describe the manner in which the *Principles* is written.

James's first suggestion is that instruction "be carried on

objectively, experimentally, anecdotally."[19] He is speaking of
a method of grabbing the attention of children, but we will
see him proceeding by means of the concrete and familiar in
the *Principles*, too. Objects, experiences, and stories are the
interest of the empiricist, so it is not surprising to see James
emphasize them. Yet, on the other hand, there is something
unusual, for if the aim of education—or of a text on psychology—is the learning of principles and laws, of abstractions,
then objects and experiences might be something of an odd
addition. The tone is unusual, too: anecdote suggests a
casual, colloquial approach, one not common in late nineteenth century education or in works of serious scholarship.

James's second law of pedagogy (and rhetoric) is to
develop interest in a topic by associating it with something in
which interest already exists. "Things not interesting in their
own right borrow an interest which becomes as real and as
strong as that of any natively interesting thing."[20] Foremost
among those objects in which an interest already exists, says
James, is one's own self.[21] So the teacher or writer must
engage not only the intellect but a fuller portion of the student or reader. The "personal self" of the student or reader is
invited into the process, and a consideration of his or her
"fortunes" is aroused. Again, this is an unusual approach. Not
only was the person of the student not usually a concern of
teachers in the late nineteenth century, but the "personal
self" of a reader is often ignored by a writer. In making the
reader central to his manner James is doing something
extremely distinctive and important.

Parallel to the second law is a third, the importance of the
personality of the teacher-writer. "Above all," he states, "the
teacher must himself be alive and ready, and must use the
contagion of his own example."[22] The difference between
the dead lesson and the fertile one is the liveliness and
engagement of the teacher. "Anecdotes and reminiscences
will abound in her talk; and the shuttle of interest will shoot
backward and forward, weaving the new and the old
together in a lively and entertaining way."[23] The successful
teacher-writer offers entertainment in order to communicate
truths, a commonplace of rhetoric reaching back to Aristotle

though one followed so seldom in philosophy and theology that it may seem that James is urging that a text become a romance. Certainly, that is how Ernest Jones saw James's writing, and it may not be too irrational a notion. In addition, James identifies the pleasure of the text not only with qualities of that text, but with the presence of the writer in it. What gives fertility is not only stories, but the writer's own stories: his or her anecdotes and memories. And it is not just the weaving of connections, but the writer's weaving of those connections, according to who he and the audience are. So much personality in something that is ostensibly didactic is, again, unusual and unexpected, like the use of the concrete.

Finally and most importantly, James suggests "novelty of order, and ruptures of routine."[24] The method is that of change. He is urging that expectations be broken. He would not allow his audience to become habituated. In a similar vein, he suggests that "the subject must be made to show new aspects of itself; to prompt new questions; in a word, to change."[25] This is the core of James's method and manner: the rupture of the expected. As I've indicated from the start, it seems to lie latent in all the methods he advocates: the use of the concrete—of objects, experiences, and anecdotes—and the prominent inclusion of personality, both that of the student-reader and the teacher-author, are not what one expects in a classroom of the late nineteenth century or in a text dealing with an abstract and philosophical topic like psychology.

Now, we must wonder if this rhetoric of James's merely acts to engage attention and interest, whether it is only a tactic, or whether it has a more substantial meaning. This, in fact, is the question of the meaning of manner. Is narrative merely a useful means of communicating events, or does it function more profoundly to orient readers in the world? Are different manners equivalent means of communicating synonymous contents? My hypothesis thus far has been that the style of a work is an element of worldmaking, that it goes beyond the subservience of rhetoric to message. I would claim that James's emphasis on the person of the reader and the writer, on the concrete and experiential, on the pleasure of the text, and on change are not "merely" aspects of manner but create content.

What James advocates must be seen in the context of what an audience expects. He seems to equate fertility with the unexpected, with violations of conventions. The usual lesson or the usual textbook is well-known in its impersonality, its abstractness, and its use of accustomed categories; subjects are viewed in accustomed ways. James's lesson breaks with the expected. A smooth, that is to say, a boring lesson or reading is unlikely when we enter Professor James's book or classroom. There would be a continuous jumping from the abstract to the concrete, from the impersonal to the personal, from the single view to the multiple. The student-reader is involved because he or she just isn't sure what to expect next. Whatever comes next is certain to be out of the ordinary. And this manner that ruptures the expected helps create a different orientation toward the world in a reader.

James suggests a method that breaks with the expected in particular ways: by using personality, multiplicity, and, closely related, inclusion. It isn't just that James would have a teacher speak about those, though that is true; the teacher must also speak *by means of* those. The *manner* uses personality, multiplicity, and inclusion. Writing is populated. It is shot through with personality. "Imagine entirely leaving the human out in a history of literature," he wrote to Henry in 1867.[26] James cannot imagine leaving it out of the classroom or a text on psychology. Writing also uses *more*: more personalities, more examples, more illustrations, more points of view, tending, perhaps, toward excess, as it pulls more in. The ideal seems to be an inclusionary manner: one that has many manners, perhaps in a stylistic *tour de force* like the Oxen of the Sun section of *Ulysses* where Joyce imitates one prose style after another—from Sallust to Thomas Malory to Dickens and Carlyle—through nearly fifty pages. James himself does not go that far, but the Joycean method is not that different, indicating yet one more way in which Joyce paddles in the Jamesian stream.

The point is not that the Jamesian text would be stylistically "fancy," but that its manner is aimed at readers and it has a constructive effect on them. It becomes one element in worldmaking—and an important one at that. We cannot say exactly what such a form does for worldmaking until we look at the manner of the *Principles* in detail.

Formal eclecticism

In turning to the *Principles* we meet the "old medieval lumber," as James himself described it, indicating not just his belief that it would soon be outmoded, but that the book is a considerable pile, an "enormous rat," in terms of size and untidiness.[27] He would trim it in the shorter version of 1892, but that is decidedly not the same work, for the *Principles* could not be streamlined greatly and remain the same masterpiece. Its ungainliness is one of its assets.

The overall design of the *Principles* is not unique, and while not streamlined, not terribly misshapen, either. Its chapters are much the same as those in textbooks on psychology by Alexander Bain, James Sully, James Baldwin, and others published in the period. Bain and Sully have sections devoted to nerve physiology. Attention, conception, association, memory, sensation, imagination, perception, reasoning, movement, instinct, emotion, and will are standard topics. If there is anything unusual about the chapter divisions, it is the inclusion of the section on the stream of thought, an idea original to James. Also unusual is the range of topics covered, for none of the textbooks on psychology of this period has the scope of James's. But, as we've said, James values inclusiveness.

Yet if the reader of the table of contents of the *Principles* isn't encountering something that is especially new, that reader certainly finds him or herself in no ordinary work once the reading of the text is begun. The principle characteristic of the *Principles* is its formal eclecticism. That is to say, it is not a work that is written in one expository form, but in a multiplicity of forms, some of which may be common and appropriate in a work of this kind, but many of which are not.

Without being quantitative about it, the single manner

that comprises the greatest proportion of the *Principles* is a very straightforward analytic, expository style. James defines; he distinguishes; he explains; he argues. So the first chapter of the book opens with a definition of psychology, a list of the phenomena appropriate to the science, an account of common ways of unifying those phenomena, a criticism of those procedures, and a case for including physiology in the consideration of psychology. There is no chapter in the book that does not contain a fair amount of such standard exposition. If there had been more of it, Charles Pierce might not have been so critical of the book for its "idiosyncrasies of diction and tricks of language."[28] A reader of the book might also have felt on ground that was more familiar, though the reader might also have read less of the *Principles* and certainly would have come away less impressed and less affected.

But such a manner is what we expect in a critical, scientific work. As much as any literary genre, the scientific text follows cultural conventions. If we were to apply Alastair Fowler's list of characteristics that define a literary "kind," we would find that the genre of the textbook is well established and the analytic expository manner definitive.[29] The "representational aspect" is discursive (certainly not narrative or dramatic). The external structure is according to chapters, arranged by topic. The size and scale are characteristically large and encompassing. The text is also recognizable by its values, a cool and deliberate desire for objective knowledge, though *desire* is far too warm a word. In fact, since attitude can also mark a kind, we find that the detached, analytical manner of the *Principles* is definitive. Use of the passive voice is common, and where the impersonal third person is not used, the impersonal "we" is found instead. Lexical range also characterizes the textbook: it is exact, polysyllabic, latineate, lacking in the expansions of the figurative. In addition to characteristics whose presence marks a kind, a kind might equally be defined by the characteristics that it does not have. Aside from lacking most figurative language, the text has no metrical structure, no occasion, no mise-en-scène, and no character or action types. It is amusing to imagine a textbook having any of these characteristics, being written in verse or on the occasion of a marriage or funeral, being spoken by shepherds or farmers or containing combat among heroic figures. It is also alluring to think of these additions, considering the austere demands that the basal analytic manner makes. But if a text had a typical metrical pattern, occasion, setting, or character, we would most certainly perceive the work as being something other than a textbook.

Most writers of texts are as desirous of avoiding the austerities of analytic manner as readers are. One manner that is commonly affixed to the analytic is the presentation of other theorists. This manner seems to me to be a considerably different one since it introduces a different voice. Analysis gives the impression of solitary mastery, presenting the voice of one decisively, infallibly making statements, as though the speaker were the unmoved mover. Quotation, on the other hand, populates a text, opening a social dimension. There are then possibilities of interaction, of agreement and disagreement, of plurality. With James, there are so many other voices—the *Principles* as a whole has over two thousand citations[30]—that it is not so much a matter of occasional quotations augmenting the basal voice as of relegating the authorial voice nearly to the status of one among many.

It is characteristic of the *Principles* that on the first page James should turn from the stance of solitary discourse to the dialogue that lies embedded in reference. All but four lines of James's first page are devoted to other views, the "orthodox 'spiritualistic' theory of scholasticism and of common sense" and the associationist theories of Herbart, Hume, the Mills, and Bain. True, James finds weaknesses in both positions, but he discounts neither. Spiritualists and associationists live on through the fourteen hundred pages, never completely absorbed, never completely banished by the authorial voice.

The same is true of many individuals in the *Principles*. James presents the views of an enormous number of psychologists, philosophers, physiologists, educators, clergymen, astronomers, physicians, economists, explorers, naturalists, journalists, and others. Often enough he disputes what they say, but more often he presents their views without imposing a magisterial authorial presence. A remarkable instance is the book's second chapter, "The Functions of the Brain," which presents the numerous and acrimonious disputes among physiologists investigating how the brain functions by studying the disorders created either by accident or by the scalpel. James summarizes areas of agreement, and he criticizes various positions, but to a surprising extent he allows the disputes to stand. Flourens disagrees with Hitzig, Ferrier, and Munk who disagree among themselves while Goltz agrees with Flourens. "Terrible recriminations" take place between Ferrier and Brown and Schafer, "Ferrier denying that Brown and Schafer's ablations were complete, Schafer that Ferrier's monkey was really deaf."[31] Elsewhere, "the quarrel is very acrimonious," between Munk and Goltz and Luciani. In fact, James notes that "the subject of localization of functions in the brain seems to have a peculiar effect on the temper of those who cultivate it experimentally.[32]

The acrimony of the second chapter accentuates the presence of others in James's book, but there needn't be dispute for the presence of others to be felt. One blatant and frequent means is simply through direct quotation, and there are prodigious instances in the *Principles*. The longest passages come from fellow investigators: 4 1/2 pages from Helmholtz (plus a page-long note from Lotze and Stumpf), 6 pages from Francis Galton, and *13* from "the pen of my friend and pupil Mr. E. B. Delabarre."[33] There is also the testimony of patients concerning hallucinations, alternate personalities, automatic writing, and other phenomena. They remind one of the many first person accounts in the *Varieties*. I would distinguish them from the quotations from Helmholtz, Wundt, and other scientists and scholars since they do not echo the voice of James's own discursive analysis, but are formally different kinds of writing. The passages from the hundreds of other psychologists, philosophers, and physiologists are of precisely the same kind as what I have called James's own basal manner in the *Principles*. They are discursive, analytic, detached, controlled, whereas the first-person accounts are, above all, narratives—but we will look at them more closely in a moment. The point I wish to make here is that James's frequent and often lengthy quotations populate the *Principles* with voices that are similar to his own analytical voice, for they are of the same generic kind.

The many narratives of the *Principles* are of a very different kind, and they add a contrasting and potentially disorienting construction. The quoted accounts of those who experience hallucinations, automatic writing, and other unusual occurrences might not be as typical as the narrated illustrations that James gives so frequently in the book. Consider the following section taken from the chapter on habit:

> When we are proficients [in any habitual action] the results not only follow with the very minimum of muscular action requisite to bring them forth, they also follow from a single instantaneous "cue." The marksman sees the bird, and, before he knows it, he has aimed and shot. A gleam in his adversary's eye, a momentary pressure from his rapier, and the fencer finds that he has instantly made the right parry and return. A glance at the musical hieroglyphics, and the pianist's fingers have rippled through a cataract of notes. And not only is it the right thing at the right time that we thus involuntarily do, but the wrong thing, also, if it be a habitual thing. Who is there that has never wound up his watch on taking off his waistcoat in the daytime, or taken his latch-key out on arriving at the door-step of a friend?[34]

The list of illustrations does not stop there, six more following in the paragraph, but if I were to include them I would soon approach the scale of James's own quoting. What I wish to point out is the mixing of two different kinds of discourse, an observation in the analytical mode (and another, four sentences later), and vivid narratives of occurrences. The difference between the two is very sharp. In the narratives we are suddenly in a sort of writing in which the concrete and particular is important, not the abstract. Size and scale are much smaller. The attitude is warmer, more personal. The values are not knowledge but experiential accuracy and aptness in expression. Character and action are essential. They are all, in fact, narrations of people performing actions. There is a beginning, a middle, and a conclusion. There is coherence and closure. There is a situation, tension,

and resolution. I do not wish to give an exhaustive characterization of narrative, only to point out that these illustrations
are strikingly different from the analytical passages.

And there is a multitude of narrative illustrations. Some
describe experiences the reader has had. "On being suddenly
awakened from a sleep, however profound, we always catch
ourselves in the middle of a dream."[35] Others concern
James's own experiences. "A young woman who had been
writing automatically was sitting with a pencil in her hand,
trying to recall at my request the name of a gentleman whom
she had once seen."[36] Yet others are stories of third parties.
"In a railroad accident to a travelling menagerie in the United
States some time in 1884, a tiger, whose cage had broken
open, is said to have emerged, but presently crept back
again, as if too much bewildered by his new
responsibilities."[37] This is a book that is rich with illustrations
of the many psychological principles and phenomena discussed, and the great bulk of the illustrations are narratives
that mix a new and different manner into the book's brew.

Of equal strength with the analytical and the narrative is
characterization, for not only is the *Principles* populated
implicitly by the voices of other investigators or by characters
involved in actions in the narratives, but James seems to take
a great deal of delight in directly describing character types.
There is the comical depiction of the German experimental
psychologists as "prism, pendulum, and chronograph-
philosophers" with "spying and scraping . . . deadly tenacity
and almost diabolic cunning," and who simply cannot be
bored.[38] There is the professor "who will poke the fire, set
chairs straight, pick dust-specks from the floor, arrange his
table, snatch up the newspaper" to avoid preparing a class in
formal logic.[39] There are also "those insufferably garrulous
old women, those dry and fanciless beings who spare you no
detail, however petty, of the facts they are recounting."[40] It is
tempting to multiply examples, in Jamesian fashion, particularly since so many of James's characterizations are so well
drawn. Let me just add one more, of the hundreds of
instances, since it is so fine. In speaking of the emotions of
the self, James gives a perfect portrait of smugness. "In self-

satisfaction the extensor muscles are innervated, the eye is strong and glorious, the gait rolling and elastic, the nostril dilated, and a peculiar smile plays upon the lips."[41] It is a description less like Henry James than perhaps Dickens, and wonderfully evocative.

These characterizations, again, are distinct from the other modes contained in the *Principles*. At times they can be quite close to the narrated illustrations, but most often they are part of nothing narrated; no action takes place so there is no plot, however minor. They are purely depictions of character. I will not yet address the question of how these characterizations function in the book since the interaction of all these modes must be discussed in some detail. For now I only wish to point out that characterization is another kind of writing, and one distinct from analysis, quotation, and narrative.

There are also a number of somewhat specific literary kinds found in the *Principles*; I'd like to look at four: the vision, the meditation, the hymn, and the exhortation. I wouldn't want to suggest that James consciously uses these kinds; my interest isn't so much in origins as in effects, in what the effect on readers may be of the manner in which the *Principles* is written. James's writing has a great variety of shapes, however they may come about.

The vision occurs when James discusses the components of the self. He emphasizes their importance by summoning up a vision of what life would be like were one of the selves destroyed. As with the other more literary forms, the narratives and characterizations, these visions of annihilation are done with considerable flair, though perhaps to the point of being somewhat florid. James begins with the straightforward declaration that the loss of a particularly valued material object can result in the "shrinkage of our personality, a partial conversion of ourselves to nothingness." Then comes the vision of that state:

> We are all at once assimilated to the tramps and poor devils whom we so despise, and at the same time removed farther than ever away from the happy sons of earth who lord it over land and sea and men in the full-blown lustihood that wealth

and power can give, and before whom, stiffen ourselves as we will by appealing to anti-snobbish first principles, we cannot escape an emotion, open or sneaking, of respect and dread.[42]

Loss of a valued object—a manuscript or an entomological collection are James's examples—is not all that rare, and thus the shrinkage of personality is not. But his hyperbole creates a condition that is anything but common. He uses an exalted diction and figures that are much larger than life to depict a future that seems drawn from myth or seen in dream or ecstasy. The depiction of a feeling of loss becomes a vision of a fall, and not unlike visionary literature in the Bible or perhaps *Zarathustra*. It is the depiction of a future catastrophe that approaches the apocalyptic.

James's discussion of the "spiritual self" involves two religious genres, the hymn and the meditation. As I mentioned, James feels that there is no single self but a multitude of selves, some of which are material selves, others social selves, and the final the spiritual self. The first two sorts he defines in a more or less conventional way and illustrates them profusely. The spiritual self is more elusive, and James seems to use a circumscription of the topic, much as he does in the *Varieties* when defining religion. That is, he does not pin the definition but moves about the topic, writing *around* it, to indicate where and what the spiritual self is. The hymn to the spiritual self and the meditation on it are two of the ways in which this "writing around" takes place.

He states that the spiritual self is the "inner-most centre within the circle, [the] sanctuary within the citadel," and he asks; "Now, what is this self of all the other selves?" After some indirect indications, he moves to praise.

> It is what welcomes or rejects. It presides over the perception of sensations, and by giving or withholding its assent it influences the movements they tend to arouse. It is the home of interest,—not the pleasant or the painful, not even pleasure or pain, as such, but that within us to which pleasure and pain, the pleasant and the painful, speak. It is the source of effort and attention, and the place from which appear to emanate the fiats of the will. . . . Being more incessantly there than any other single element of the mental life, the other elements end by seem-

ing to accrete around it and to belong to it. It becomes opposed to them as the permanent is opposed to the changing and inconstant.[43]

It is a subtle hymn, principally because it uses so much scientific language of perceptions, sensations, effort, and attention, and so little poetic language. But the character that James gives to the spiritual self is much like that of a kingly God. It welcomes or rejects imperiously. It presides; it gives or withholds. It is the source. From it come fiats. Finally, it is the permanent among the inconstant. And while the passage seems to be purely descriptive, what it describes is so powerful and admirable that the passage is, in fact, laudatory. Finally, the repetition of "It" ("It is. . . . It presides. . . . It is. . . . It is. . . . It becomes. . . .") gives the passage the rhythm of a hymn. Replace the neuter pronoun with the masculine or feminine and the hymnic qualities will stand out quite plainly.

James's meditation is not of the clearly religious sort found in St. Ignatius Loyola or in seventeenth-century poets like Herbert, Crashaw, or Vaughan. Nonetheless, he does engage in a deep reflection, an examination of himself at a private and profound level. Moreover the meditation is an attempt to reach and describe the spiritual self, which he has previously praised in hymnic terms. James emphasizes that the spiritual self can be felt, that it is something "with which we have direct sensible acquaintance,"[44] and in his meditation he attempts to describe what he feels when he is aware of it. So James's meditation is not on a religious theme but on a feeling that has religious import.

> First of all, I am aware of a constant play of furtherances and hindrances in my thinking, of checks and releases, tendencies which run with desire, and tendencies which run the other way. Among the matters I think of, some range themselves on the side of the thought's interests, whilst others play an unfriendly part thereto. The mutual inconsistencies and agreements, reinforcements and obstructions, which obtain amongst these objective matters reverberate backwards and produce what seem to be incessant reactions of my spontaneity upon them, welcoming or opposing, appropriating or disowning, striving with or against, saying yes or no.

There follows a remarkable meditation on the bodily feelings associated with the activities of the spiritual self such as willing, attending, reasoning, and consenting.

> In the first place, the acts of attending, assenting, negating, making an effort, are felt as movements of something in the head. In many cases it is possible to describe these movements quite exactly. In attending to either an idea or sensation belonging to a particular sense-sphere, the movement is the adjustment of the sense-organ, felt as it occurs.[45]

As the hymn to the spiritual self was a peculiar mix of the scientific and the psalmic, James's meditation is a combination of the religious meditation and scientific observation. What makes it different from a report of observations in a conventional scientific paper or text is the sense a reader has that James is meditating as he's writing, the internal nature of the observation, and the object of the meditation, the spiritual self. None would be found in scientific writing. All are characteristic of such religious meditations as Pascal's *Pensees*, St. John of the Cross's *Dark Night of the Soul*, or Donne's *Devotions*.

In addition, James's attitude toward the topic of his meditation is considerably more like the meditation than the scientific observation. As Frances de Sales writes,

> Sometimes we consider a thinge attentively to learne it's causes, effects, qualities; and this thought is named studie, in which the mynd, is like locustes, which promiscuously flie upon flowres, and leeves, to eate them and nourishe themselfes therupon: but when we thinke of heavenly things, not to learn but to love them, that is called to meditate; and the exercise thereof Meditation; in which our mynd, not as a flie, by a simple musing, nor yet as a locust, to eate and be filled, but as a sacred Bee flies amongst the flowres of holy mysteries, to extract from them the honie of Divine Love.[46]

James is a "sacred Bee" in his meditation. We can catch his reverence for the spiritual self, his concern to touch it, not simply to consume it. While James's intent is to learn, it is also to love.

The contrast with the other manners of writing in the

Principles is strong. The writing is personal and introspective. It attempts to capture something very elusive not by the rigors of analytic logic or descriptive recall but by the careful touch of self-reflection. And for the reader, entering the meditation means entering a manner (and a world) that is markedly different than the one he or she just left in this book.

One final manner in this sample is the sermonistic exhortation that ends the chapter on habit. James has a physiological explanation of how habit works, he has spoken quite forcefully of the "ethical implications of the law of habit," and he has offered a number of maxims to enable readers to make their habits their allies instead of their enemies.[47] By themselves, of course, the second and third forms introduce yet other generic kinds to the *Principles*: the treatise on theoretical and practical ethics. But after presenting the fourth maxim ("Keep the faculty of effort alive in you by a little gratuitous exercise every day"), James uses the concluding paragraph of the chapter to urge his readers—especially the young ones—to follow his advice. He cites a proverb by way of warning. "The hell to be endured hereafter, of which theology tells, is no worse than the hell we make for ourselves in this world by habitually fashioning our characters in the wrong way." He follows with platitudinous sayings. "We are spinning our own fates, good or evil, and never to be undone. Every smallest stroke of virtue or of vice leaves its never so little scar." He reminds readers of the omniscient eye that follows their actions: "a kind Heaven may not count [every fresh dereliction]; but it is being counted none the less. Down among his nerve cells and fibres the molecules are counting it." Then he frankly exhorts, with the hortatory subjunctive, "Let no youth have any anxiety about the upshot of his education . . . if he keep faithfully busy each hour of the working-day." And concludes with a promise. "He can with perfect certainty count on waking up one fine morning, to find himself one of the competent ones of his generation."[48]

We could go on and on listing the generic kinds or manners that comprise the *Principles*, but I want to add just one more before turning to how these forms are put together. Among the analyses, quotations, stories, characters, visions, and hymns of James's textbook, there lie scattered a multitude of literary excerpts and allusions. In the first paragraph of his preface, he quotes Goethe in hopeful excuse of the *"vieles"* that the book includes, and he concludes the second volume by noting that the more one tries to understand the mind, the more one perceives "the slowly gathering twilight close in utter night." Between are passages from Jane Austen, Robert Southey, Ovid, Thackeray, Job, and many more. The quotations are short, a few lines at most—certainly never to the length of the passages from scientific works. They are also generally more distinct from the body of the text, sometimes in French or German or quoted in verse or in a block, and standing out, as the Russian Formalists say, for being different, unfamiliar, estranged from ordinary prose. Whether the excerpts and allusions are identified or not, they are identifiable as different, as literary, so a reader moves into the literary when he or she runs across them, opening out into Goethe or Tennyson or Shakespeare or Emerson from the rather different confines of the text to the point that quotation began. Moreover, the reader encounters a number of different literary voices. More, perhaps, than Wundt differs from Helmholtz, Tennyson, or Emerson differs from Dante or Homer or Shakespeare. So while James doesn't really range over literature with the breadth of Ezra Pound—he concentrates on his fellow Victorians and on the classics—a reader must move about considerably nonetheless.

The fact that James mixes a great variety of literary forms in the *Principles*, that a reader encounters James in his analytic voice; dozens of other investigators in their analytic voices; quotations from a wide swath of literature; narratives of hundreds of different characters performing hundreds of different actions; characterizations creating a vast milling throng within each volume; hymns, meditations, exhortations, and visions and more—this variety might be interpreted in a number of ways.[49] Most immediately it may seem similar to James's theory of the fringe in consciousness. Nothing in consciousness, he says, is discrete. We are never aware of an object absolutely

unconnected with anything else: in his famous example, we
do not hear thunder but "thunder-breaking-upon-silence-and-
contrasting-with-it," as well as linked to memories, desires, personality, and a panoply of associations. "Relations," James
notes, "are numberless."[50] Similarly, we might say, there is not
a solitary manner in James's writing: no manner stays put in a
proper compartment, but is linked to numerous others. How
we speak now is linked by a fringe to how we have spoken
already, to manners of speaking that we have heard or read.
We can keep them discrete, but there is something appropriate in one pulling others along for company.

According to this view, the mixture of styles in the *Principles* is a kind of mirror of the stream of consciousness, and
the way in which James's textbook is written would be
chaotic for being like the domesticated chaos of consciousness.[51] Yet that would be a false argument, I think, for what
was chaotic about consciousness was not that there was a
fringe but, rather, how that fringe, and the other characteristics of consciousness, functioned. A collection or a mixture is
not a chaos. As I argued in the opening chapters, nothing is
inherently chaotic. Instead the chaotic is relative: there must
be a contrast or challenge to something that is more stable or
structured. To use the example from chapter 2, a kayaker
may see a rushing river as a quite orderly pattern of eddies,
hydraulics, and chutes, while I might see it as utterly chaotic
in comparison with a smoothly flowing stream. Milton's *Paradise Lost* is a "panoply of literary forms" according to Barbara Lewalski's analysis, but we would not, I think, be correct in calling that work chaotic. For neither Milton nor his
epic challenge anything that is more structured or stable. In
fact, the work creates stability by its generic comprehensive-
ness and is in accord with, not challenging, contemporary
theory and practice.[52] So the mere existence of a mixture of
modes does not make a chaos.

Mikhail Bakhtin's discussion of generic inclusiveness in
the novel helps illumine this matter. He emphasizes that the
novel incorporates a vast variety of genres, "both artistic
(inserted short stories, lyrical songs, poems, dramatic scenes,
etc.) and extra-artistic (everyday, rhetorical, scholarly, reli-

gious genres and others)." In fact, he notes that any genre could be included in a novel and most have been.[53] Yet Bakhtin does not see the novel as aspiring toward a completeness, toward the stability of a final collection of forms, but toward inconclusiveness and indeterminacy. It does this because of its "dialogic" quality. The genres included in the novel are parodic: they are aimed against official genres for being established, bounded, and hardened. The incorporated genres in the novel laugh at what is fixed, much as James scoffs at "old fogeyism." The dialogic aspect of the novel also takes place among the genres included since they offer a multiplicity of often conflicting viewpoints and world views. They constitute a "heteroglossia," a Babel of voices clammering within the end-pages of the novel. These "heteroglot, multi-voiced, multi-styled and often multi-languaged elements" create inconclusiveness and indeterminacy in relation to both what is outside the novel—other genres, social structures, objects, persons—and what is inside it.[54] Bakhtin sees the novel taking part in what he terms the centrifugal forces struggling toward "decentralization and disunification" and against the centripetal forces that move toward unity and centralization.[55] Wayne Booth calls this centrifugal movement one "dispersing us outward . . . into a seeming chaos . . . [of] fluidity and variety."[56]

The novel's heteroglossia is not congenial to fluidity and chaos because it is a mixture but because of its dialogic character: because of how its elements interact with what is inside and outside the book. What is important is how the genres function, not their number. And that is what we have to look at next in the *Principles*: how the variety of forms work, which means the effect that they have on the reader. For one whimsical enough the *Principles* might be classed a novel because of the heteroglossia that exists in it, but it is unclear whether it would function dialogically as Bakhtin says a novel must.

Interactions of forms in the principles

There are probably no representative chapters in the *Principles*, but let me choose two sections from the book so that it can be sampled somewhat fairly in looking at the mixtures it contains.

The five-page presentation of "Rivalry and Conflict of the Different Selves" in the chapter called "The Consciousness of Self" is a fairly dense section illustrating the quick oscillation of manners that often takes place in the *Principles*.[57] The point James makes in these pages is that we must choose among the many selves that we have, and how we handle that choice determines our "self-feeling": whether we feel satisfied with our selves or not. The four pages contain several statements concerning, as it were, the laws governing multiple selves, and analysis of the operation of those laws. For example, James states that nature constrains us to stand by one self and abandon the others, and, after giving an example of multiple selves, he explains how many of them must conflict. Yet statement and analysis together comprise no more than about twenty sentences, or perhaps one-fourth of the entire section. The remainder is composed of characterizations, narrations, and quotations in support of the observations, with a swift movement from manner to manner that allows each to stand but a brief period in a reading.

James uses himself as an example of one having multiple, conflicting desires.

> Not that I would not, if I could, be both handsome and fat and well-dressed, and a great athlete, and make a million a year, be a wit, a *bon-vivant*, and a lady-killer, as well as a philosopher; a philanthropist, statesman, warrior, and African explorer, as well as a "tone-poet" and saint.

Shortly thereafter he again uses a depiction, that is, a characterization of himself as one who has staked all on being a psychologist and has relinquished all pretensions to knowledge of Greek. These personal depictions alternate with statements of a scientific sort, and are followed by an extensive list of characterizations of those who have also given up certain pretensions or are in need of the relief such would give. We meet the lover, the Bostonian devotee of the symphony, and those striving to be young or slender, and James finishes with the story of a man who lost all in the Civil War and rejoiced for it.

The next brief paragraph is devoted to Carlyle who quotes "the wisest of our time"[58] urging renunciation: we have a voice in a voice in a voice in that passage. From there to the end of the section we find the same oscillation as earlier: a general statement, this time saying that we cannot appeal to a person unless we address one of his or her actual selves, followed by a flood of characterizations and quotations—diplomats and monarchs, a dialogue from Epictetus (again a voice within a voice within a voice), James assuming the voice of a narrow person, a quotation in Latin from Terence, James assuming the voice of a sympathetic person, and a quotation from Marcus Aurelius—interspersed with occasional statements and analysis.

It is a whirling transit for readers, and it seems to me that the oscillations must keep those readers aware that, like Dorothy, they are not in Kansas anymore; that is, that this is not a genre with which they are acquainted. Each of the elements is known well enough, and in each of them a reader could be comfortable enough, but the sudden changes undermine familiarity. The manner seems to attack "consistency-building," as Wolfgang Iser calls it.[59] In this case it isn't just making sense of the novel (how we evaluate Alworthy in *Tom Jones* is Iser's example), which is undermined by subplots, unreliable narrators, multiple perspectives, and so forth, but how we become oriented in the work. Just as a reader might discover what genre he or she is in, it disappears and another takes its place that then is displaced itself by another destined to fall and be replaced by another, and so forth, and so on. The result would seem to be two different sorts of disorientation: a reader does not find him or herself within an identifiable textbook and then the genres that do arise are replaced both swiftly and with often strongly contrasting substitutes. Iser's phrase, bombarding the formulated gestalten, seems to be an apt one.[60]

It might be helpful, once again, to contrast James's procedure in this section with that in ordinary exposition. Iser mentions that texts that develop an argument or convey information depend on connectability.[61] It is desirable that a reader not be lost, that he or she be guided, in fact, along

rather precise routes so that the text end in being either persuasive or effective. "The multiplicity of possible meanings,"
Iser says, "must be constantly narrowed down by observing
the connectability of textual segments."[62] Iser contrasts this
desire for "good connection" with fictional texts that break
up connectability in order to multiply possibilities, to dislo-
cate the reader's ordinary expectations, and to force the
reader to construct his or her own connections.[63]

Clearly the *Principles* is more like Iser's fictional texts
than it is like exposition, and that is in good part due to the
dialogic character of the genres included in it. It would be
wrong to say, of course, that James's book multiplies possibilities indefinitely—but it would be wrong to say that of a
novel, as well. James argues against a physiological determin-
ism, a Lockean sensationalism, and many other positions.
Fielding does not let a reader conceive of Alworthy as a char-
latan, a hypocrite, or a rake. But *Tom Jones* or any novel
tends to open possibilities by breaking up "good connection," and so does the *Principles*.[64] James's book does it in
what it says by advocating a pluralism, empiricism, and
nascent pragmatism, and it does it in *how* it speaks by multiplying genres that rupture expectation, by not remaining in
the analytic expository manner, and then by the suddenness
with which the genres succeed and by the strong contrast
among them.

James suggested in *Talks to Teachers* that "ruptures of
routine" and "novelty of order" help to maintain attention.
We see in the *Principles* that breaking expectations has
become the manner of his writing. It is not just that there is a
panoply of forms in the text, but that they are arranged in
such a way that, in Iser's terms, consistency and connectability are broken. A reader is not readily oriented, for each genre
lacks continuity with the next—a next that comes all too
soon. And if the form of what we read is as important as I
believe it is, strongly providing us with orientation in the
world, then the frequent switching of genres must be a significantly disorienting experience. It is in this sense that James's
writing would seem to be dialogic, and the multiplicity of
forms chaotic: because they challenge a more stable or more

orderly generic structure. Another way to put this is that the result of gestalt bombarding is not only disorientation but reorientation, but that is a topic that must wait until later.

Multiple voices

If James's section on the conflict of selves contains such a clash of genres, is that equally true of the *Principles* as a whole? Mightn't it be a manner particular to that section and appropriately tailored to its topic: a clash in manners parallel to a clash among selves? In order to counteract any such impression, I'd like to look at a quite different and longer section, that on the neurological changes associated with the formation of habits and on the practical consequences of those changes.[65]

Though these fifteen pages have two dense sections like those we just looked at, the changes among genres are less abrupt. But what is more noticeable is a characteristic of James's manner that I have not emphasized, and that is the degree to which the multiplicity of forms is actually a multiplicity of voices. In part this was implicit in my brief survey of formal kinds in the *Principles*. The quotations from philosophers, physiologists, psychologists, clergymen, botanists, adventurers, and so forth appear in the text as voices of various individuals. James's use of characterization adds a teeming crowd to his pages. Yet in addition to these, *all* of the generic kinds in James's book create personalities, many of them directly speaking in voices. The result is that the formal diversity of the book is experienced as an encounter not only with different sorts of literature but with different sorts of people. The *Principles of Psychology* is a collection of voices as much as it is a collection of theories or a collection of generic kinds. Considering James's own emphasis on personality—his collection of photographs so that theorists were not just ideas but people, his belief that differences in philosophy (or choice of deity) were to a large extent differences in temperament—the presence of voices in the *Principles* is not surprising. Not surprising but profound.

The voice that is most important in the *Principles* is

James's own, both because it speaks most of the lines, and because it causes a reader to hear the others in the book as voices, too. For example, in discussing whether thoughts have parts, James presents himself as intellectually pinned both by those who feel that such parts correspond to the parts of physical objects and those who feel that such parts correspond to individual neurological "molecular facts." "What shall we do?" he laments. "It may be a constitutional infirmity, but I can take no comfort in such devices [as religious awe and hegelianism] for making a luxury of intellectual defeat. They are but spiritual chloroform. Better live on the ragged edge, better gnaw the file forever!" It is a dramatic, even melodramatic speech, and it does much to create a person out of the authorial voice in the *Principles*.[66] Ordinary expository style may be largely impersonal, but James succeeds in making his heard as a genuine voice. And that is not only by appending passages that are of a different generic kind, as in this example, or in the case of the vision, meditation, hymn, or exhortation earlier. Within James's most controlled, exact, and analytical prose lie irrepressible personal notes, as in his use of slang—"the upshot of it," a "'rule-of-thumb' thinker," and getting "'stuck'" all exist in the opening pages of the chapter called "Reasoning."[67] His examples are also frequently anecdotal, as when he illustrates the "Proofreader's Illusion" by recounting:

> I remember one night in Boston waiting for a "Mount Auburn" car to bring me to Cambridge, reading most distinctly that name upon the signboard of a car on which (as I afterwards learned) "North Avenue" was painted. The illusion was so vivid that I could hardly believe my eyes had deceived me.[68]

One gets the sense, in fact, that a fair biography of James could be written purely from the views of him that we're given in the *Principles*. The pleasures of smoking, the birth of children, the events of vacations, the obligations of a parent's last will and testament, the chores of teaching: if ever we're justified in inferring an author from a text (and I believe we are), we're justified in this text.[69] As James urged in *Talks*, "The teacher must himself be alive and ready, and must use the contagion of his own example."[70]

A considerable result of the transformation of James's expository and analytical passages into a personal voice is that the passages from other psychologists, philosophers, and so forth, tend to be heard as voices, as well. The chapter on habit is a fine example of this process. James is busy explaining how habits are formed physiologically: it is a fairly dry topic, yet he manages to make the explanation both understandable and his manner somewhat light by the use of imaginative metaphors—the brain is encased in a "boney box," the nerves are "drainage-channels"—and by maintaining the personal voice he has established in the opening three chapters. He caricatures "Mechanical Science" that "in her present mood" will "set her brand of ownership" on the study of habits. He frankly admits that his explanation of the formation of new habits is "vague to the last degree." He also says he has noticed in learning a tune that skill increases after a rest. When he follows with a long quotation from William Benjamin Carpenter ("Dr. Carpenter writes:"), we tend, I believe, to read the passage as a voice, too, even though it has none of the warmth of James's writing. We simply take it as another kind of a voice, one that is cool, dry, and detached. After two and a half pages of the remote Dr. Carpenter, James returns briefly but with a characteristic colloquialism: "Dr. Carpenter's phrase . . . expresses the philosophy of habit in a nutshell." G. H. Schneider follows rather abruptly, without announcement or introduction, and in a different voice than Carpenter's or James's, to be succeeded after a page by James, briefly again, then Henry Maudsley ("Dr. Maudsley says:"). Schneider speaks twice more in these pages and Carpenter three times, once quoting a biography of the magician, Jean Eugene Robert-Houdin, in which Robert-Houdin himself is quoted addressing his readers. "This . . . will probably seem to my readers very extraordinary; but I shall surprise them still more."[71]

The voices do not entirely cease when James begins drawing the ethical implications of habit, but the manner shifts from the alternation of expository voices to the rather dense presentation of narratives and characterizations by way of illustrating the consequences of habits good and bad. "Habit a second nature! Habit is ten times nature!" James quotes the Duke of Wellington, then cites Thomas Huxley's story about a man who "suddenly called out 'Attention!'" and caused an ex-soldier to drop his dinner. A crowd of people and animals follow, riderless cavalry horses, trained dogs and oxen, released prisoners, an escaped tiger, the fisherman and deckhand at sea in the winter, "the miner in his darkness," the countryman in his log cabin, the young commercial traveler, the young doctor, the young minister, the young counselor-at-law, and more. These last do not speak: they are presented in narratives and characterizations, interspersed, as before, with James's more or less scientific statements. "Habit is thus the enormous fly-wheel of society, its most precious conservative agent."[72]

The same multiplicity of forms exists in this section on habit as it did in the other section we analyzed. A reader is similarly prevented from achieving a comfortable orientation in a familiar genre since the genres change. This is more true of the latter part of our sample, where the narratives, exposition, and characterization oscillate rather quickly.

In the earlier part, we have an example of Bakhtin's "heteroglossia," a collection of voices. Again, merely having many quotations does not make the manner of the *Principles* "chaotic." Any book that uses quotations is not thereby "chaotic." What is important is that the quotations are read as voices, as speech. As Michael Holquist writes in his introduction to *The Dialogic Imagination*:

> Other genres are constituted by a set of formal features for fixing language that pre-exist any specific utterance within the genre. Language, in other words, is assimilated to form. The novel by contrast seeks to shape its form to languages; it has a completely different relationship to languages from other genres since it constantly experiments with new shapes in order to display the variety and immediacy of speech diversity.[73]

Now, obviously the *Principles* isn't shaped by speech to the degree that a novel is. The sort of speech is different in the *Principles* than in a novel, and however much quoting there may be in James's book, it doesn't have the prominence of speech in a novel. Nonetheless, the *Principles* is a collection of persons, characters, and voices, a collection larger than in any of Henry James's novels if only because the *Principles* is so long and the characters are generally so briefly done. And what makes the heteroglossia centrifugal in a novel, makes it centrifugal in the *Principles*, as well. If voices are not disciplined by form, then the reader's ear gives them the autonomy and integrity of any voice. We respect voices, we listen to them, for behind voices are persons, and culturally we are compelled to respect persons as ends. The textbook is a very loose form, organized solely by rather large topics. So the voices in the *Principles* are not disciplined by the form. Rather, they speak, and James's book has the shape that it does as a result of that speaking.

Of course, not every textbook has the shape or the effect of James's. In great part this is because other texts do not transform the authorial manner into a personal voice, make their quotations into voices, or populate the book with characters or with the other forms that help to fragment the whole. But also it is because most authors exercise far stricter control over their work than James does. Most textbooks are dominated by the omniscience of the author or by the omnipotence of the factual. There cannot be heteroglossia because one voice subsumes all others. James is much more benign. Let there be no mistake: it is his book. But he allows others to participate in the expression. And it is because he makes words into voices and allows those voices to speak that the *Principles* has a dialogic quality, a quality that compels a reader's attention to be more dispersed, less unified, and hence more chaotic.

Nonetheless, the *Principles* is not purely a collection of conflicting voices. It does not pull together the five notable viewpoints on each topic, and allow them to go at it verbally. The manners and the voices do not produce "utter confusion and disorder"; the dialogic aspect is not, I think, experienced by a reader as threatening. The voices disperse attention; they do not utterly break it. The generic forms do not purely disorient; they initiate reorientation.

Domesticated chaos: image streams

To this point I have emphasized the disparities in the *Principles*: the heteroglossia and the multiplicity of forms that can change suddenly. But now we need to look more carefully and decide if the form of the *Principles* shapes readers in a way that is indeed congruent with the content of the book. That is, the form of James's textbook can be seen to have a "chaotic" effect on readers because it challenges and dissolves the orientations implicit in its many forms and voices, so the experience of the reader moves against the established, the relatively formed, ordered, and static. But is that chaotic effect more like the "domesticated chaos" of *The Principles of Psychology* or more like the harsher, more threatening chaos of *The Varieties of Religious Experience*?

First we need to clarify how specifically the form of a work can shape its readers. It seems to me to be unlikely that the manner in which a work is written can determine with precision how a reader will orient him or herself in the world. It seems more likely that the form interacts with a number of other factors, such as the more explicit content of the work, the recollection of other works of that kind, the personal and cultural attitude toward the form or competing forms, and, very importantly, religious and philosophical attitudes and beliefs. The *Iliad* read in late twentieth-century America surely shapes readers differently than it did in Periclean Athens or in late twentieth-century New Guinea. There would seem to be no fixed calculus of reader response. Yet a form would seem to provide a reader with a range of persuasive options that are simultaneously narrowed by other factors.

What, then, is the range of options for the form of the *Principles* today? Are they more similar to domesticated or disruptive chaos? It will not come as a surprise that I think an argument can be made for domesticated chaos. I mentioned in chapter 3 that the difference between the chaotic in the two books is in the degree of violence (and the consequent attitude toward it): the stream of selves *dissolves* while the extramarginal material *bursts* the boundaries of the self.[74]

Domesticated chaos is valued for its ability to loosen restrictions, avoid the ponderous, and combat rigidity. Extreme chaos is dangerous, creating anguish by undermining the stabilities that support life. It is abrupt and wrenching.[75] To see whether the effect of the *Principles'* manner on a reader is more like the dissolving or the bursting, I'd like to take a look at one last characteristic of the book's form.

All readers of the *Principles* are impressed, no doubt, by one stylistic peculiarity that makes the book an especial pleasure to read, and that is James's streams of images. The *Principles* is as full of these streams as Frost's "Hillside Thaw." It seems the usual convention today to have three examples or illustrations: one is simply not convincing, two is slightly insufficient, three clinches the argument, while four is superfluous. James tends to begin with four and commonly runs to eight or more. In speaking of illusions, he writes, "The boy playing 'I spy,' the criminal skulking from his pursuers, the superstitious person hurrying through the woods or past the churchyard at midnight, the man lost in the woods, the girl who tremulously has made an evening appointment with her swain, all are subject to illusions of sight and sound." Discussing the variety of conscious states, he says, "Now we are seeing, now hearing; now reasoning, now willing; now recollecting, now expecting; now loving, now hating; and in a hundred other ways we know our minds to be alternately engaged." In speaking of stimuli to attention, he mentions "strange things, moving things, wild animals, bright things, pretty things, metallic things, words, blows, blood, etc., etc., etc."[76] Virtually every page of the book has such lists.

Like the stream of consciousness, these image streams involve both continuity and difference. Each item of a list is different from the others, yet all are collected together in a continuous flow. The fact that they are all in one list tends to undercut disjunction and replace it with conjunction. All are illustrations of one principle, phenomenon, observation, experiment, or other class ("illusions of sight and sound," stimuli to attention). There is also an internal logic that links the items (the associations in the "strange things" list are especially fascinating). At the same time, the distinctness of each item is not lost, for James takes care to include relatively disparate items. He is inclusive in his lists. It has been said that the use of the catalog in such American romantics as Emerson and Whitman indicates their belief in divine plenitude. "Exuberance, profusion, endlessness, surprise—these are the most obvious qualities of Transcendentalist enumerations and the principle that underlies them."[77] The same could be said of William James whose lists greatly resemble the catalogs of Emerson and Whitman. In all, the relationship between continuity and difference in these streams seems similar to James's view of the pluralistic universe. There is "neither a universe pure and simple nor a multiverse pure and simple," he states in *Pragmatism*, for there are both definite conjunctions and definite disjunctions.[78]

The harmonious view seems to predominate in the image streams of the *Principles*. Even in the most extreme example there seems to be as much conjunction as disjunction. Perhaps that extreme is found in James's attempt to evoke the "simply given order," the plenum that we cannot perceive because it is an "utter chaos." "While I talk and the flies buzz, a sea-gull catches a fish at the mouth of the Amazon, a tree falls in the Adirondack wilderness, a man sneezes in Germany, a horse dies in Tartary, and twins are born in France."[79]

While the list may seem utterly disjointed on first look, its items are joined, first, by autobiographical links: James's trip to the Amazon with Agassiz, his vacations spent in the Adirondacks, his travels in Germany and France. Only Tartary is a wild card, and one might wager that a look at James's casual reading at the time would turn up a connection there. But even for a reader unfamiliar with James's past, there is continuity. There is the theme of life and death joining the elements: the flies (suggesting decay) and the sneeze (portending illness) being the only obscure links. There seems to be common imagery of air, flight, and arrival. No doubt we could discover more connections, but the point, I think, is made: James's lists are more harmonious than not. They are *streams*.

In fact, we might see the image streams as orienting readers toward the most domesticated form of the chaotic in the

Principles; they seem to be more harmonious than the mixture of forms or the heteroglossia. The differences between the elements in one of James's lists are relatively minor compared to the differences between voices or genres. We can have lists of narratives or lists of quotations or lists of theories or lists of characters or simply lists of nouns, verbs, or adjectives, but all items within those lists are of the same kind. Consequently there is not the same violation of orientation. There is an operation of the chaotic, since James's illustrations tend to run a wide gamut. Thus a reader's imagination moves through a greater variety than he or she is accustomed to. Lawrence Buell notes that the catalogs of Emerson and Whitman are sometimes seen as "literary anarchy" expressing terror and chaos, and argues that they are intended to mirror a "fluid but cohesive universe."[80] What tames James's enumerations is the fact that the variety and differences are subsumed within the overall list. The image stream seems to be a technique whereby differences and variety are integrated: the chaotic is domesticated.

The domesticated chaos of the image streams seems more typical of the *Principles* than not. The disjunctions and disorientations of the multiplicity of contrasting forms and voices tend more toward the model of the image streams than toward the strong chaos we might find in a work by Beckett. Why is that? To answer that question we need to examine how reorientation takes place for a reader of the *Principles*.

Re-orientation

We mentioned in the first chapter that a pure chaos, that is, absolute formlessness, is inconceivable, for we must conceive through some form or other. Every chaos is formed, and so it might be a Timaean primordial whirl or an Ovidian undigested lump or Miltonic warring elements, a Stevensian tropical freedom or a Chopinian mere knot. So, too, there is no sheer disorientation, however confusing the mixture of forms in a book or the cacophony of voices. A reader always succeeds in making some sort of sense, in orienting him or herself to the world of the book, knowing what sort of up is up, what sort of down is down.

Such reorientation is automatic, yet James explicitly invites it by advocating that his readers approach his book introspectively. "Introspective Observation is what we have to rely on first and foremost and always," James states with emphasis in his chapter called "The Methods and Snares of Psychology."[81] He calls upon his readers to verify whatever he says by their own introspection.[82] Frequently he addresses his readers directly. He includes them in his examples and illustrations. He invites them to perform thought experiments. Of course, as Wolfgang Iser points out, the role of the reader is just another role in a work. It is by no means the only role that a reader assumes.[83] My point is only that James pulls his readers into his book somewhat more directly than most works of serious scholarship. He is more concerned, as Perry says, to "reach out to them, touch them, and feel their response."[84] Readers do not orient themselves because of that, but it facilitates their orientation. The *Principles* becomes a book somewhat harder to ignore or to read passively.

A reader of the *Principles* is disoriented since he or she is not in an expected genre and since the multiple genres and voices of the book continuously engage and then disappear, surplanted by the claims of new voices and forms. A reader, however, makes sense of this multiplicity and change. The usual manner of reading cannot continue since there is no generic continuity, and, at the same time, the multiple forms and voices cannot simply be left and forgotten when they cease. The reader demands comprehensive sense, requires a comprehensible bridge across the text's differences, needs there to be a more or less coherent world in this one book. The "gaps" that exist within the text, to use Jerome Bruner's word (Iser calls them "blanks"), prompt the reader to create bridges. Iser terms this process the "wandering viewpoint": a reader is occupied with one perspective after another in a novel, while still aware of the others as a "background." Gradually, Iser says, the reader synthesizes a view of the world that is more or less congruent with the desires of the author who has, after all, arranged the perspectives of the characters, narrator, plot, and virtual reader in order to influence the reader. It seems to me that a construction like this takes place not only among articulated perspectives, such as we get in the voices in the *Principles*, but also among the generic forms.

What makes the reader's construction different in the *Principles* than in many works is that in James's book the construction involves a species of the chaotic. While what Iser and Bakhtin say of the novel makes it sound very much like a form with much in common with the chaotic, a novel can certainly be conservative or value stability and order. Certainly most works in philosophy or psychology do not challenge expectations through their styles as James's does.[85] The *Principles* quite sharply requires that worlds be taken apart or abandoned before new ones are made. This rubble becomes the raw material for the construction which follows.

As Nelson Goodman points out, constructing a world begins with another world, one that already exists.[86] He says that there are at least five ways in which new worlds are made out of old: composition and decomposition, weighting, ordering, deletion and supplementation, and deformation.[87] The *Principles* seems to use several, by first correcting or decomposing the old and then by supplementing inclusively. This is the crucial aspect of how this book is written. It *adds* manners of writing. The *Principles* takes apart the old by multiplication and juxtaposition and then adds all together into an inclusive view. This means, of course, that a reader does not abandon narrative, argumentation, or characterization, Helmholtz, Carlyle, or the Duke of Wellington. The exclusive worth of each is discounted; the order and claim of each alone is undercut as it is quickly succeeded by another form or challenged by another voice. In their place (unless explicitly denied by the authorial voice, as Spencer often is), the orientations of each voice or form are added.

Whether a form creates a sense of domesticated chaos or one of disruptive chaos seems to depend on whether the elements (genres, voices, or items in a list) predominantly clash or build. There will be no chaos of any kind if there is a firm structure among the elements, be that imposed by authorial voice, the "facts," or genre. In that case there would be no challenge to structure, order, or form. But in a work that is dialogic, whose elements are in tension with expectations or with one another, the sort of chaos that is inculcated depends on the degree of tension. If it is wrenching, making reorientation extremely difficult, then we have disruptive chaos. If the elements can coexist, if any one form or voice can survive constant challenge to exist in a plurality, if we have the dissolving of forms and voices coexisting with their survival, then the chaotic has been integrated. It has been domesticated. The *Principles of Psychology* seems to be such a work.

According to this view, the voices and forms in the *Principles* exist in streams, much as the illustrations and examples do. None is allowed to be distinct but is continuously challenged by the multiplicity of others; each is washed in the free water of manner. But each also performs its own function; each orients the reader in the way that it alone is capable of doing. Hence we have the same oscillation between the creation of boundaries and their dissolution that we have in the stream of consciousness.[88]

Chaos out of cosmos

Ralph Barton Perry remarks of James that "he enlivened everything that he touched, fertilized every idea that passed through his mind, carried a blazing torch in all his meanderings, zigzags, and circles."[89] Here again we have man, matter, and manner, though with a decided emphasis on the man from this colleague, friend, and biographer. The man is the source of life, giving it to ideas, and carrying light even in his peculiar peregrinations. Yet what if James was a "blazing torch" in part *because* of those "meanderings, zigzags, and circles"? What if those chaotic wanderings did not demand extraordinary creativity but give it?[90] My proposal is that *The Principles of Psychology* is an extraordinary work, a masterpiece, not merely because of what it says but how it says it. John Dewey remarked that the *Principles* "exploded the ancient superstition that works of science, to be authoritative, had also to be deadly dull."[91] Surely we can see now that James's *Principles* is not only served by its manner, it is achieved by it: by being, as James himself noted, "a richly colored chunk."[92]

Why does the *Principles* have its peculiar shape? Why the "meanderings, zigzags, and circles"? Why is it written in this odd genre? A genre realist might respond that it mirrors something real, that our experience really is such a kaleidoscope or that consciousness is. Such a person would clash with a thinker like Stephen Crites who feels that our experience is sequential and hence best mirrored by narrative. Both would disagree with current linguistic philosophers who argue that we cannot get behind our symbols to discover what reality is *really* like. In Richard Rorty's words, we never encounter reality "except under a chosen description."[93] According to these thinkers, not only is the mimetic dictum that art must imitate nature wrong, even the notion that nature imitates art "is too timid a dictum." Nelson Goodman's bold conclusion is that "nature is a product of art and discourse."[94] If these thinkers are correct, the *Principles'* "meanderings, zigzags, and circles" create a corresponding nature. As though it were an odd, modern demiurge, the *Principles* creates a chaos out of cosmos.

5

"Instruction from the Living Voice": Creating Chaos in *The Varieties of Religious Experience*

Introduction

As we have seen, the manner in which *The Principles of Psychology* is written leads readers to perceive themselves and the world as having a shape approximating what I term *domesticated chaos*. The multiplicity of generic forms and voices and the often abrupt change from one to another disorient readers much as a film might disorient viewers if they expected a historical romance and saw, instead, a succession of images of varying lengths from comedy, cartoon, documentary, and political debate. The viewers' experience might be described as chaotic because they are not oriented in an accustomed or stable way. They keep looking for the historical romance, and, in fact, keep receiving sufficient elements of it to maintain their expectations. Yet with each clip from Woody Allen or the Nixon-Kennedy debates they enter a different world with different assumptions about who we are and what matters. Relative to a viewing of any one of those film genres, their experience is chaotic.

With *domesticated* chaos the reorientation that takes place is not wrenching. The multiplicity of genres and voices do not predominantly clash; they build. Old genres and voices—in Nelson Goodman's terms, *old worlds*—are decomposed because of juxtaposition, but then they are supplemented. The newly constructed world of this book is an inclusive one. In the end, the manner in which the *Principles* is written is as integrative and healthful as the matter of the book (as healthful, I would speculate, as the man who wrote it wanted to be himself).

What of the *Varieties*? This work is characterized by a

dangerous and disruptive variety of the chaotic. Individuals are thrown into confusion by the evil of the world or by their inability to sort the world into a meaningful order. A "divided self" is formed, which is marked by continuous and arduous strife. There is nothing domesticated or integrated about such chaos, nothing streamlike or fluid. It is often agonizing, always extremely difficult. And even when the resolution of the religious crisis arrives, when "firmness, stability, and equilibrium" are achieved in conversion, it takes place as an *annihilation* of the old by the new. How does the style of the *Varieties* manage to shape a reader's perception of self and world in an analogous fashion?

The answer, I believe, is that the *Varieties* is at once more tame and more dramatic than the *Principles*. It has all the elements of the older work—the multiplicity of genres, their often abrupt succession, the multiplicity of voices, the image streams—so that a reader unaware that the two were written by the same man could recognize an identifiable style. Yet crucial differences in the characteristics of each of these manners and in the relations among them produce a different effect on a reader. The *Varieties* does not create a coherent, inclusive whole. Rather, the voices of this book are abnormal, acute, unstable, discordant: voices of extreme instances of extreme occurrences, and a reader cannot integrate them into the cohesive whole possible in the *Principles*.

Generic multiplicity

While there is considerable generic diversity in the *Varieties*, it is not as great as in the *Principles*. In that sense, the manner of the *Varieties* is tamer than that of the earlier work. There are few characters used as illustrations, few narratives, and fewer of the specific generic kinds (hymns, meditations, visions, etc.). The latter do exist. There is at least one lament, numerous lyric passages, satires on Saint Teresa of Avila and Saint Louis of Gonzaga, a hymn to alcohol, extravagant praise of poverty and of saints, and one "dark saying."[1] At base there exists the expository genre, the manner of the investigator who is detached and analytical, though this manner is complicated by a more personal voice in the *Varieties*.

Occasionally the genre mixture is dense, as it was in the *Principles*, although there is not the extravagance or exuberance of that book. For example, early in the chapter called "Saintliness," there comes an argument between the impulses and the inhibitions ("'Yes! yes!' say the impulses, 'No! no!' say the inhibitions"), followed by James's observation that few people are aware how constant this argument is. He addresses his audience and imagines how they would behave in the room if alone, each becoming "more 'free and easy.'" Next he observes how inhibitions can disappear, moving to an anecdote of a dandy in public with shaving cream on his face because of a fire, the illustration of a woman in a nightgown saving her baby, and the contrast of two character types, the self-indulgent woman and the mother. The paragraph ends with a reference to the British physician, James Hinton, writing about sacrifice and joy.[2] Within thirty lines, the text moves from personification to authorial observation to the direct address of the audience to the imagining of a situation to another authorial observation to narrative anecdote, narrative illustration, a pair of characterizations, and the paraphrase of another investigator.

Other specific genres in the *Varieties*—laments, lyrics, satires, and so forth—lie in a similarly dense mixture, as do nearly all the narratives and character depictions. Moreover, within these somewhat limited sections of the *Varieties*, quite a number of catalogs occur, again without quite the vitality of those in the *Principles*. Shortly after the paragraph I just summarized, James mentions that in individuals "with an inborn passion" there is no "inner friction and nervous waste" from the struggle with inhibitions.

> To a Fox, a Garibaldi, a General Booth, a John Brown, a Louise Michel, a Bradlaugh, the obstacles . . . are as if non-existent. . . . Given a certain amount of love, indignation, generosity, magnanimity, admiration, loyalty, or enthusiasm of self-surrender . . . our conventionality, our shyness, laziness, and stinginess, our demands for precedent and permission, for guarantee and surety, our small suspicions, timidities, despairs, where are they now?[3]

It's a fine instance of James's cataloging, but relatively rare in the *Varieties*.

In all, there are perhaps seven or eight sections of the *Varieties* that are similar to the dense mixtures of the *Principles*, and those sections have nearly all of the characteristics that the earlier work had. Were this all, the experience of a reader of the *Varieties* would be much like that of a reader of the *Principles*, and I might be hard pressed to explain what I take to be an important difference between the works: the radically different function of the chaotic in each. Yet the *Principles'* forests of mixed modes rose from the lengthy level stretches of James's scientific, expository style and voice, a manner of writing broken, as well, by the generous quotations from his fellow investigators. It is what replaces these in the *Varieties*—James's new voice and the new quotations—which make reading the later work a far different matter than reading the earlier. What is of lasting importance to a reader is not the relative tameness of the genre mixtures but the forcible drama of the book's voices.

Multiplicity of voices

James begins his lectures and book by extolling "the experience of receiving instruction from the living voice."[4] He is speaking about those Europeans who lecture in American universities, yet his phrase, "the living voice," makes it seem much more important than that. The phrase, in fact, is pleonastic: What else is the voice but alive? It's also a synechdoche: the voice isn't living; the human behind the voice is. James's figure couples two matters that are of great importance to him and to this work: the voice and life. If we are to receive instructions from his book, it will be because of the voices that speak from its pages and because of the vitality of those voices. The multiplicity of living voices makes the *Varieties* something of a drama, though an unusual one.

The leading voice in this drama is ostensibly that of James, himself.[5] As in the *Principles*, the authorial voice in the *Varieties* is occupied with arguing a case. Nonetheless, that voice succeeds in being heard as a living voice to an even greater degree than was true of the earlier book. We might want to say that is because the book began as a lecture series, so there was a living voice. But as a lecturer James could have chosen to be impersonal: we've certainly all heard lecturers whose voices are decidedly dead. What is it, then, that makes a reader hear a living voice in the pages of the *Varieties*? I said that James's voice becomes personal in the *Principles* due to such irrepressible notes as his use of slang, anecdote for illustrations, and generic kinds that seem directly spoken. In the *Varieties*, a reader feels that he or she is encountering a person—not an investigator, a reasoner, or an observer—because the matters discussed seem so personally important to the speaker.

The most impassioned words come when James deals with the sick soul, a predicament that he seems less to describe than to advocate. For example, after presenting healthy-mindedness and the sick soul as dominant ways of reacting to life, James personalizes the alternatives by imagining an argument between them. He asks: "In our own attitude, not yet abandoned, of impartial onlookers, what are we to say of this quarrel?" His answer quickly abandons impartiality for he asserts that evil simply *is*. "The normal process of life contains moments as bad as any of those which insane melancholy is filled with. . . . Our civilization is founded on the shambles, and every individual existence goes out in a lonely spasm of helpless agony. If you protest, my friend, wait till you arrive there yourself!" It could be a quotation from Tolstoy, Bunyan, Luther, or any of the others whose words from the depths James presents. The *Varieties* contains many whose selves are divided or whose souls are sick, but one seems to inhabit all of its pages, and that is the author himself. He alone is not confined to a blocked quotation, although, of course, he is there too.[6]

James often assumes the voices of others, as he did in the *Principles*. In the earlier work he spoke as a suicide, a Stoic, a polyp, and many others; in the later book he speaks for both the healthy-minded and the sick soul, but with a keen difference in intensity. When speaking of those whose souls have the "sky-blue tint," he's most likely to use the first-per-

son plural. "At all costs, then, we ought to reduce the sway of
that [pining, puling, mumping] mood; we ought to scout it in
ourselves and others and never show it tolerance."[7] On the
other hand, James's presentation of the view of the sick soul
often shades off so subtly into the voice of such a one, that it
is hard to tell where the voice shifts. Is it James the investigator who says that the happiness of the healthy-minded is pre-
carious, that "he might just as well have been born to an
entirely different fortune. And then indeed the hollow security! . . . Is not its blessedness a fragile fiction?" Evidently, the
investigator in these pages is nearly indistinguishable from
the voice who feels that "pain and wrong and death must be
fairly met and overcome."[8]

There are many, of course, who feel that one who inves-
tigates must be objective, that is, must be more like an object
than a subject. In order to speak of eternal things, the heart
must be consumed away since it is sick with desire and fas-
tened to a dying animal, as Yeats writes in "Sailing to Byzan-
tium." James takes an opposite point of view, both in his theory and his practice. As he argues in the *Varieties*, "It is
absurd for Science to say that the egoistic elements of experience should be suppressed. The axis of reality runs solely
through the egoistic places—they are strung upon it like so
many beads."[9] As this book indicates, we need to include the
subjective—or, as I prefer it, the personal—not just in what we
study but in how we study it. And therefore James speaks as
a sick soul.

Yet James speaks in another voice, as well. One aspect of
healthy-mindedness that James's authorial voice frankly
advocates and endorses is the strenuous life, which is pecu-
liarly similar to the sick soul, for both involve a struggle that
can amount to a species of heroism. Evil can often be con-
quered by a change of attitude. "It can so often be converted
into a bracing and tonic good by a simple change of the suf-
ferer's inner attitude from one of fear to one of fight."[10] For
the healthy-minded individual the struggle is successful: evil
disappears. The sick soul cannot be as successful for always
"the skull will grin in at the banquet."[11] Yet in both cases we
can hear an authorial voice urging the value of the struggle.

Some people, he says, cannot "live on smiles." "Passive happiness is slack and insipid, and soon grows mawkish and intolerable. Some austerity and wintry negativity, some roughness, danger, stringency, and effort, some 'no! no!' must be mixed in, to produce the sense of an existence with character and texture and power."[12] In the complete passage, James presents both sides, those who say yes and those who say no, but he speaks far more vigorously for those who live strenuously.[13]

A reader of the *Varieties* encounters a different sort of author than does a reader of the *Principles*. In neither case is there only a detached, impersonal, purely analytical voice, for we clearly hear the voice of a particular person with concrete concerns, a specific past, and vivid feelings. But in the *Varieties* the topics *matter* so much more to the voice. The voice *believes* in the fact of evil, and in the profundity of the experiences of the sick soul, and it *insists* that explanations that do not take evil into consideration will not do. That voice (or perhaps it is yet another one) is committed to vigorous effort and urges the moral equivalent of war. This voice makes greater claims on a reader than the voice in the *Principles*. I mentioned in the last chapter than any voice claims our attention, that we are culturally compelled to treat it as an end in itself, and for that reason the multiplicity of voices disrupts the continuity of the text, unless, as Bakhtin says, the voices are disciplined by form. I am not certain how the voice we have here could be disciplined by a form. For we care a great deal about this voice that is struggling with matters that can lead to great suffering. A reader becomes involved with this voice to a degree that may eclipse concern with the analysis of religious experience. James's discussion of religion is, of course, brilliant and extremely influential, but it is easy to emerge from the book primarily moved not by a theory but by a man.

And James's is not the only voice in the book. That, in fact, is the most important fact about the manner in which this book is written. It contains a variety of living voices that break the margins of a reader's awareness with stories that are, perhaps, more extreme and affecting than James's own.

As readers we are seized, perhaps transfixed as the wedding
guest is by the mariner in Coleridge's *Rime of the Ancient
Mariner*, but in this work there is not one bright-eyed man
confronting us but dozens.

James's use of concrete voices runs parallel to his concern for the dangers of classification. In his opening chapter
he distinguishes an existential from a spiritual judgment. The
first involves classifications: religious passions, for example,
are classed psychologically or biographically. They lose their
uniqueness and become one example of a general kind or
they are explained as the result of a cause. A spiritual judgment, on the other hand, involves significance. Regardless of
how a religious passion may be classed, we judge it according to what it means to us, according to the values that have
worth for us.[14] James seems ambivalent about these two judgments. On the one hand, his task in this book is to treat religious experiences as psychological phenomena, "comparing
them with other varieties of melancholy, happiness, and
trance," and offering an explanation for conversion according to a theory of the subliminal self.[15] James's purpose is to
classify religious experience. On the other hand, James is
acutely aware of the oversimplification, dogmatism, and
reduction that can result from such "existential judgments."
"It is true," he writes, "that we instinctively recoil from seeing an object to which our emotions and affections are committed handled by the intellect as any other object is handled."[16] We feel that anything that is enormously significant
to us must be *sui generis*, and not comparable to anything
else.[17] It seems that James finds a solution to his ambivalence
in combining his classification and analysis with the presentation of vivid examples—balancing the abstract with the concrete.

Yet if it is calm balance that James seeks in combining the
two, he does not achieve it, for the two coexist in considerable tension.[18] The opposition is formed by the character of
the voices that James presents. Unlike the often lengthy quotations from psychologists, adventurers, naturalists, philosophers, journalists, and so many others in the *Principles*, these
quotations do not create a harmonious summation of views.

James himself describes them as discordant, exalted, and abnormal. He has decided to choose his examples from those where "the religious spirit is unmistakable and extreme." They are "one-sided, exaggerated, and intense."[19] Though James presents these experiences as being not different in kind from the more ordinary, more tame manifestations, nonetheless, as they appear in the pages of the *Varieties*, they are extraordinary.

The first occurs seven pages into the text of the *Varieties* and it marks the book as a work out of the common. It is a passage from George Fox's *Journal* recounting his summons by God to denounce Litchfield, England as "THE BLOODY CITY!" That one passage says enough. James certainly doesn't exaggerate when he calls Fox "a psychopath or *detraque* of the deepest dye." Fox hears the voice of the Lord numerous times, he sees rivers and pools of blood in the streets and markets, and he walks through the city, "crying with a loud voice, WO TO THE BLOODY CITY OF LITCHFIELD!"[20] Frankly, it is an account that is hard for a reader to reconcile with his or her own experiences. The passage describes a world that is far different from the ordinary world of the reader: few of us hear God speak, have visions, or feel called upon to denounce a city publicly. Consequently, the movement from the preceding text to that of Fox's testimony involves an extreme shift that we might call a radical reorientation.[21]

That seems true of nearly all quotations from the "great-souled persons wrestling with the crises of their fate."[22] In the chapter called "The Reality of the Unseen," some accounts are so uncanny that they resemble passages from Poe. "[A]bout September, 1884, . . . I had the first experience. On the previous night I had had, after getting into bed in my rooms in College, a vivid tactile hallucination of being grasped by the arm." That experience certainly seems uncanny enough, but it isn't the object of this narrative. On the next night

> suddenly I *felt* something come into the room and stay close to my bed. . . . It stirred something more at the roots of my being than any ordinary perception. The feeling had something of the

quality of a very large tearing vital pain spreading chiefly over
the chest . . . and yet the feeling was not *pain* so much as
abhorrence.[23]

Others are less uncanny than simply extraordinary and moving, such as that by a clergyman who speaks of the night
when "my soul opened out, as it were, into the Infinite, and
there was a rushing together of the two worlds, the inner and
the outer . . . I stood alone with Him who made me, and all
the beauty of the world, and love, and sorrow, and even
temptation."[24]

The accounts are of various types. Those that recount
experiences of the healthy-minded are often narratives of
what might be considered miraculous cures. They begin with
descriptions of physical and emotional ailments. The suffering is nearly always interrupted—interestingly enough—by a
voice in these accounts: either the afflicted speaks some
piece of Mind Cure wisdom to him or herself, or it recounts
that "I suddenly heard as it were these words."[25] The narration concludes with the disappearance of the symptoms.

While the accounts of the healthy-minded are "exalted"
because they are miraculous, those of the sick souls are
extreme for involving such vivid anguish. Luther confesses "I
am utterly weary of life." Father Gratry recounts "such a universal terror that . . . I suffered an incurable and intolerable
desolation, verging on despair. I thought myself, in fact,
rejected by God, lost, damned!" And a patient in an asylum
calls out: "Where is the justice in it all! What have I done to
deserve this excess of severity? Under what form will this
fear crush me? What would I not owe to anyone who would
rid me of my life!"[26] The quotations in the chapters on the
divided self and conversion are similarly affecting in the
severity of the suffering communicated in so direct and personal a manner. They are also startling in their accounts of
transformation, where they occur.

These narrations and reflections rupture the continuity of
the text in an abrupt manner. They wrench a reader away
from the argument that James is developing in his pages.
They even refuse to be of a kind with the other accounts.
They insist, I believe, on being unique and on making an

uncompromising demand on the attention and emotions of a reader. They do this for three reasons. First, they are voices. Each of these accounts speaks directly from the pages to the reader. There is no narrator to be an intermediary. A reader hears the voice of a person undergoing suffering or salvation, and, as I have argued, a voice has enormous weight with a reader. Second, the accounts are extended. A sentence integrated into James's prose could be integrated into the world of the text. A voice could be muffled by argument, description, and analysis if it were sufficiently brief. But these voices speak for 10, 20, 30, or more lines. They establish themselves in that span, and a reader can be pulled in. Third, the voices speak of extreme situations, with extreme passion, and extreme eloquence. These are people with "a superior intellect and a psychopathic temperament," and unless their tales are too exaggerated and violent to hold us at all, they hold us unusually well. Again, Coleridge's *Rime* seems to be a close analogue. Like the wedding guest who is stopped by one with "long grey beard and glittering eye," we "cannot choose but hear."

Interruption by a voice, in fact, exists as a pattern in the *Varieties*. Not only are there dozens of extended quotations that interrupt James's text, but within those accounts there are numerous cases where the speaker is spoken to, be it by God, Jesus, an angel, or an unidentified voice. Stephen H. Bradley sees the Savior who says to him, "come" (like Jesus in Mark's Gospel), and Bradley's conversion takes place. Mr. S. H. Hadley vows never to take another drink and "something said, 'If you want to keep this promise, go and have yourself locked up.' . . . I did learn afterward that it was Jesus [who spoke]." Henry Alline is wandering in the fields, "lamenting my miserable, lost and undone condition . . . [when] the following impression came into my mind like a powerful, but small voice. You have been seeking, praying, reforming, labouring, reading, hearing and meditating, and what have you done by it towards your salvation?"[27]

James's own psychological theory makes use of a similar mechanism. He explains the occurrence of visual hallucinations, voices, automatic actions, or obsessive ideas as

"'uprushes' into the ordinary consciousness of energies orig-
inating in the subliminal parts of the mind."[28] The margin of
ordinary consciousness *bursts* and material from beyond the
margins rushes into the field of consciousness. It seems to me
that the voices in the *Varieties* behave in a similar fashion for
readers. James's descriptions of religious experiences, his
classifications of kinds of religious individuals, his psychological explanations for various religious phenomena exist
within a field for a reader. They are what one might expect in
a work of this kind. The voices of those in an "acute fever,"
with "abnormal psychical visitations" and "exalted emotional
sensibility" speaking of terrible anguish, miraculous transformation, and, often, tremendous bliss interrupt that expectation. They burst through the margins of ordinary discourse,
wrenching a reader from his or her accustomed orientation
in the text.

Disruptive disorientation

But is this disorientation any different from that which took
place in the *Principles*? I said in the previous chapter that the
Principles disorients readers since they are not in an
expected genre and since the multiple genres and voices of
the book continuously engage and then disappear, surplanted by the claims of new voices and forms. That happens
also in the *Varieties* but with a critical difference. The difference lies in the kind of reorientation that takes place. Reorientation is a process that occurs at the same time as disorientation: a reader is confused by the alternation of genres and
voices and, at the same time, he or she makes sense—or puts
down the book. When reading the *Principles* a reader *adds*.
The exclusive claims of each genre or voice is discounted by
the contrast of the next, but the reader puts together an
inclusive view embracing them all. In terms of worldmaking
through reading, this reorientation involves correction and
decomposition followed by supplementation. But in reading
the *Varieties* a reader would not seem to add voices. Each is
too insistent on its own pain or happiness. Each is too large a
piece of a life. Each is too far outside ordinary experience.

Each is, as James says, *sui generis*. Consequently, the coexistence of these voices in the same work is—to put it mildly—extremely uneasy. In reading the first-person narratives, we can identify the characteristics that James points out. We can classify and define. But a large surplus refuses classification and cannot be integrated into the work as a whole. In fact, these voices threaten the *Varieties*. They tend to pull it apart into warring elements, refusing to come together into a coherent world. The manner in which this book is written creates a disruptive chaos indeed.[29]

It has been my experience that it is common for readers to skim through the quotations in the *Varieties*. The point, after all, is to find out what James thinks, and all these long passages from obscure religious fanatics simply get in the way. If we read them, we're forced to read them for themselves, and that can interfere with the discovery of James's thought. It is very unusual to find a reader who reads all the way through each quotation. Though these observations are merely anecdotal evidence, they indicate that this is not a work that entices readers into a satisfying world. Rather, to enter this book fully is to enter a world that is chaotic in a disturbing sense, and that is an experience readers tend to avoid.

The Varieties of Religious Experience is a book that is challenging in many ways. Unlike *The Principles of Psychology*, it is not a depiction of health, a description of the integrative functioning of the mind in its capacity to approach the inclusive richness of the teeming world. The *Varieties* concerns evil, pain, and disruption. While James sees healthy-mindedness as a legitimate stance toward the world, the aspect of it that he admires most frankly is its moral strenuousness, its capacity to be heroic. The sick soul and divided self live in turmoil, unable to come to terms with the radical evil of the world and their own despair in the face of it. Confusion and chaos are hallmarks of these individuals. The converted experience a transformation, but it comes as the bursting of a dam as they are overwhelmed by a flood from beyond the margins of the self. And those who are most exemplary among the converted, the saints, can lead lives obsessed with orderliness, fearful of the slightest sign of disorder. This is not a tranquil work, and who can wonder when James compares God to a flood and waterspout. Religious men, he states, are content to close their mouths "and be as nothing in the floods and waterspouts of God."[30] Those may, indeed, be the equivalent in this work of the streams in the *Principles*. Tempestuousness has returned, but it is neither something that terrorizes the self into paralysis, nor something to be tamed into an orderly stream. It is energizing, giving the individual the strength to be heroic or to withstand confusion, to acknowledge evil and not deny it. It is the burst flood of transformation that does not drown but creates a new life.

The manner of the *Varieties* is like a flood and waterspout, as well. The voices in this book are too strong for any bounds. They refuse to be contained as mere illustrations. They are powerful expressions of extreme experiences, and so they sweep over a reader like a divine tempest, creating a reading that is disruptively chaotic. And the "chaotic" reading is not destructive but creative, giving the reader something of value that he or she would not otherwise have.

But what is it that the chaotic gives? I believe that we must approach that question by looking at what is religious about the chaotic. Two different chaotic worlds, one domesticated and the other disruptive; two manners of writing that produce different chaotic readings. Are those worlds and those readings religious in any meaningful sense? Answering that question will be the task of the final chapter.

6
Conclusion

"Fronting life": the chaotic and religious orientation

In a letter to the philosopher George Palmer in 1900, William James uses a telling figure to describe the religious import of his philosophy.

> If our students now could really begin to understand what Royce means with his voluntaristic-pluralistic monism, . . . what Santayana means by his pessimistic platonism, . . . what I mean by my crass pluralism . . . that these are so many religions, ways of fronting life, and worth fighting for.[1]

This is by no means the only time James says that his pragmatism or his pluralism is religious,[2] but the passage helps us to understand why he does so. At the same time it gives us a fresh understanding of what a religion is: something that enables us to "front life." It seems to be an image out of James's crisis years. Life is a tempest and our craft rides it best if it's pointed into the storm. A religion points us forward by letting us know where forward is: in a word, it orients us.

Orientation involves knowing where the east is, the place where the sun rises, for from that reference point we've divided the world into quadrants and stand in an orderly relation to our surroundings. But we aren't only oriented spatially; temporally we require orientation, too. We divide time into present, past, and future, and we know which of our mental images belong to which time. Orientation does not just involve simple placement; it establishes significance and meaning, also. We're oriented relative to circumstances and to objects if we know what significance they have for us. We place ourselves relative to them. We exist in an environment that makes sense. Similarly we're oriented temporally not only if we know what is present and what is past, but if time has meaning for us.

This sense of orientation is related to James's "fronting" metaphor: it's facing a *particular* way, as a church should be oriented to the east. So a religion may orient us temporally by pointing us toward an eschaton or toward a cyclical renewal or toward events that indicate God's covenant. We're oriented relative to ourselves, to other people, to nature, to political and social institutions, to the facts and theories of our time, and to much else. In each case, we're placed, matters make sense for us, and, most importantly, we are able to move. For the purpose of knowing east is to be able to walk toward it (or toward the west, south, or north).

There are many orientations, but the ones that place us in the larger dimensions of life and death, time, sociality, humanness, and fulfilling activity are religious orientations. To be human is to be in need of orientation in these matters, and that which orients us may be called religious by definition. It has been a matter of some debate whether there is an engulfing worldview that orients us, subsuming other orientations. This view would hold that our political philosophy, our personal ethics, our view of death, and our attitudes toward love are all harmonious, as though the polarity of them all subtly pointed, say, due west. Another view, one that would likely be favored by James himself, holds that such a unified worldview is an unwarranted metaphysical assumption. Empirically we are all in what E. M. Forster calls a "muddle," and that is simply the extent of what we experience and know. Our political, social, theistic, and interpersonal views may each take hold of existence in quite different ways. If, as James says, the alternatives of monism and pluralism are matters of temperament, I would have to confess to the personal conviction that what humans think and feel coheres. But I admit, as well, that much is to be gained by not assuming coherence too quickly. As Michel Foucault warns, the assumption of uniformity can covertly oppress what is different.[3]

If that which orients us is, by definition, religious, it might seem that we are disoriented without religion: we don't know where we're going or where we've been; we don't know what is about us. In James's figure, we are driven dangerously by the tempest if we cannot front it. But I would offer that absolute disorientation is not possible, for disorientation is another kind of orientation.[4] Perhaps we feel disoriented because the world lashes or mocks or toys with us, but that is a variety of orientation, too. We are oriented and we are religious simply by being human. Disorientation is that variety of orientation in which we do not satisfactorily front life but are in intolerable perplexity, anguish, or despair. Disorientation differs from orientation purely in its relative degree of adequacy. That is not to denigrate the pain of disorientation. It is just to say that humans require orientation, and they unfailingly achieve it.[5]

The orientation that I have explored in this book is the chaotic. We have seen that it is a widespread notion in James, collecting together such terms as *fluidity*, *indeterminacy*, *multiplicity*, *fragility*, and *vagueness* in the *Principles*, and *perplexity* and *conflict* in the *Varieties*. Many have said that James's view of the world and humanity is chaotic, some considering that a defect and some a strength. My suggestion is that the chaotic is a basic term of his thought, one foundational enough to constitute a worldview. My aim in this final chapter is to discuss how chaos might function as a religious orientation. Central to that discussion is the notion of disorientation, for it is of the essence of the chaotic to flirt with it, but first we need to clarify just what orientation involves.

Orientation: scope, authority, and benefit

One current religious thinker who makes extensive use of orientation as a function of the religious is Gordon D. Kaufman. His primary purpose is to explore the role played by the Christian symbol of God "as a focus or center for devotion and orientation."[6] That analysis illumines the notion of religious orientation in three ways. First, it tells us that religious orientation requires scope. A concept of God is itself part of a world-picture, which orients us by providing us with an image of the largest dimensions. We are certainly oriented by images of smaller scope: I have a mental picture of my living room that can guide me safely through it in the night; I also have a sense of my relations with my friends that enables me to interact with them satisfactorily. But a religious orientation requires larger scope.[7] It has to do with a mental picture of the furniture of the world as a whole, or of my significance as a person and my relations with all humans.[8] Such a world-picture interprets life and the world for us, sometimes explicitly as in a philosophy or theology but more often imagistically as when we have what we might call an organic notion of life and imagine the universe as being interrelated as are the parts of a plant. We know who we are, where we are, and where we are going according to some inchoate organic image.[9]

Another aspect of orientation that Kaufman stresses is that humans seem to need a center of orientation outside of themselves.[10] Though he makes this statement concerning God, I think we can see that it applies to orientation as a whole in terms of its critical and authoritative functions. Critically, orientation would seem to involve not only the sense of where east is, but the sense of where it is not. Whatever the center (or principle) of orientation may be, it conflicts with and overrules alternatives and competing tendencies.[11] God may have a much stronger critical function than most, but any orientation must maintain itself. Moreover, it would involve an authoritative voice. Orientation would always seem to order experience decisively, dividing right from left, significant from insignificant. "Anything" will not go. So all orientations have authority, just not the extreme of authority that God has. Religious orientation per se would seem, then, to be both critical and authoritative, for a compass that meekly changes north to satisfy the whims of the walker will not orient anyone anywhere.

The third aspect of orientation that Kaufman clarifies concerns its humanizing function. Traditionally God is presented as just, merciful, caring, loving, and forgiving. God is personally interested in human salvation and actively working toward it. In less theistic terms, God indicates that evolutionary and historical tendency whereby humanity moves toward authentic fulfillment.[12] Again, aside from the distinctive orientation that God offers in Kaufman's discussion, we can say that orientation itself may be viewed as beneficial. Not only does it protect us, enabling us to "front" life, it enables us to meet life, to gain from it what can be gained, for with our senses forward we can gather life in. Thus orientation is fulfilling: it lets us be filled. It is also fulfilling in a more teleological way: we orient ourselves in order to go someplace, in order to accomplish something. We face forward in order to "fare forward," as T. S. Eliot writes in "The Dry Salvages." So orientation satisfies our ends. In both senses, then, orientation per se is humanizing.

Chaotic orientation

Gordon Kaufman argues that many religious orientations that are not focused on the symbol of God can become either idolatrous or not authentically fulfilling. If a finite end is elevated to ultimacy there is considerable potential for the dangers of the inquisitions and pogroms that have filled history. It is hard to disagree with the claim that human hubris and idolatry can have (and have had) catastrophic consequences. On the other side, despair and hopelessness can be the result if there is no symbol as powerful as that of God. If our deepest fulfillment is not grounded in reality itself, what hope is there that we are oriented in a meaningful direction?

In contrast to Kaufman, my interest is not in discovering the most fulfilling religious orientation but in exploring those orientations that people use in spite of all manner of disadvantages. There are certainly many theists in the modern world, but there are also many for whom God plays scant role as a focus of orientation. A multiplicity of orientations exists, as Kaufman points out. It seems worth exploring how they work and why they work, for they do successfully function to enable humans to "front" life and do so in ways that we can describe as fulfilling as well as harmful. I see these orientations as being much more modest than a theistic one, as being more ordinary and mundane. The extraordinary power of the symbol of God is not involved, and instead more modest symbols suffice.

What, then, of the chaotic? We have seen from Kaufman's work that humans must orient themselves religiously through an image of the world that will give them a sense of context, that their orientation is both critical and authoritative, and that it is beneficial, contributing to human fulfillment in some sense. We could add to our picture by looking at others who have written about orientation either implicitly or explicitly, particularly Kant, Schleiermacher, Nietzsche, and William James himself. But the question of whether humans can have a chaotic religious orientation can be adequately settled using the criteria we already have.

It seems clear that chaos can orient. It lets us know, first, who we are, where we are, and where we are going. The tempestuous image that was meaningful to James in his crisis years is a fine illustration. It depicts the world as an extremely dangerous and disordered place that threatens to shatter all human structures such as the will, and presents only the options of passive drift or suicide. Though we might not recommend such a view to others, it did serve to orient James during the late 1860s and early 1870s.

The *Principles'* domesticated chaos is a far more viable orientation. It integrates the challenging and dissolving power of the chaotic into consciousness. The stream of selves; the multiplicity of interests; the fringes of memory, perception, and identity; even the floodings of the neural stream are a detailed depiction of who we are. Where we are, the chaotic plenum, contains a richness from which we are cut off by our need for limitation. Finally, James seems to say that we are called to incorporate as much as possible of the wealth that the world offers: that, in a sense, is our destiny. We are most healthy, it seems, if we are most like the plenum. Not only did domesticated chaos function successfully to orient James, to allow him to "front" life, but it has, I believe become a powerful mode of orientation in the present century, whether James has been the major source of it or merely one other participant. Unfortunately there is no opportunity to develop this idea here.

Illness, once again, not health, is the focus of the *Varieties*. Its disruptive chaos is profoundly difficult without being ultimately destructive. The world is a place of evil, of the "infernal cat" and the "panting mouse," but the true problem consists in perplexity, despair, and meaninglessness.

From that chaos comes a division of the self that is resolved when integration is achieved by the annihilation of the old self by the new. James still values inclusiveness, but its price is that current selves must be burst for new, more capacious ones. The disruptive power of the chaotic seems the destiny of all who wish to grow.

In these different ways, then, chaos (or, preferably, these two chaoses, the domesticated and the disruptive) describe humans, their world, and their future. They oriented James, I feel; they have been powerful orientations in this century; and potentially they can orient us today by presenting us with world-pictures of religious scope. It seems needless to add that they are authoritative and critical since they brook chaotic interpretations and no others.[13]

The chaotic and disorientation

The third characteristic of a religious orientation raises a much more difficult question. As Kaufman says, and as Kant, Nietzsche, Eliade, James, and others have stated in their own terms, an orientation must be beneficial. In Nietzsche's words, it must be life affirming, in James's phrase, "useful to life." For Kant, it can guide us "to our true destination."[14] What, we might reasonably ask, is beneficial about a chaotic orientation? One answer might be that it is an orientation, after all, and some orientation is better than none. But while that could conceivably be an adequate answer concerning the tempestuous worldview James adopted during the late 1860s, it is far too minimal for the considered and developed views implicit in the *Principles* and *Varieties*. It also under-rates the usefulness of chaotic worldviews both historically and in the present day. To address the question of the bene-fits of chaos, we need to examine not orientation but disori-entation.

I stated earlier that absolute disorientation does not seem to be possible for humans.[15] My reasons are analogous to those I gave in chapter 1 for the impossibility of a formless chaos. According to a long line of thinkers, starting perhaps with Kant, all experience is figured; *qua* experience it is shaped. Kant claimed that it was formed by the *a priori* concepts of the understanding. Cassirer saw prior forming through symbols. Linguistic philosophers focus on the forming done by language. What we do not have, all these philosophers believe, is a shapeless experience that is only subsequently patterned. Every chaos, I concluded, is a cosmos (or Joyce's "chaosmos"). The same seems true of orientation. Aside perhaps from very early infancy and very extreme psychosis, we always have some notion of self and world. The experience of self and world is always formed *somehow*. In fact, I would claim that even early infants and psychotics are oriented if only they have an emotional attitude toward the inchoate blend of sense data and mental activity, even though they might not differentiate self from world. If an infant feels comfort or a psychotic feels rage, he or she is oriented.[16] And since that emotion encompasses all in the experience of that infant or psychotic, I would even claim that it is a religious orientation.

So disorientation is extremely rare and perhaps impossible. Nonetheless, the concept of disorientation is an important one culturally, and many concepts that are closely allied with it have been important religiously. On the disruptive or "hard" side of chaos, allied to the sense active in the *Varieties*, there is despair, meaninglessness, anomie, oblivion, and nothingness.[17] There is Pascal's fear of the infinite spaces and his sense of being lost—disoriented—within them. He trembles at the sight of "those two abysses of the Infinite and Nothing."[18] There is the centrality of despair and dread in Kierkegaard's thought, and the dizzying paradoxes that result from the nature of faith.[19] There is, also, Karl Barth's belief that humans need to be "broken," that all that exists apart from revelation is "a void and a deprivation," and that revelation is experienced as a "burnt-out crater."[20] For a long tradition of religious people, disorientation is a critical religious experience. It is savage and extreme, and however justified it may be by divinity, its intensity is not lessened. It is never tamed, never domesticated.[21]

Utter disorientation continues to be a central religious category today, both in the faith of which Pascal,

Kierkegaard, and Barth wrote, and in terms of contemporary challenges of enormous concern such as nuclearism, the holocaust, and other genocides. All of these insist on the reality of utter disorientation; they insist that all meaning of self and world, all parceling of significance, all division of universe and life into this and that are utterly gone.[22] Such absolute disorientation is, I have claimed, an impossibility. To be at all is to be oriented. Yet, paradoxically, a term like *chaos* is able to orient us, if I may use an awkward term, *disorientedly*. It tells us, "You are 'disoriented'" and it forms our experience in a chaotic shape such as those we encounter in James, Shakespeare, Hobbes, Kierkegaard, or Barth. The concept of chaos allows us to experience the unexperienceable. It allows us to be disoriented. It cannot allow us to be disoriented literally; rather it gives our experience a form that *says* it is formless. "Chaos" says that our experience has no shape to it, that it is "utter disorder and confusion," and thereby we are able to have as close to such an experience as we humanly can.[23]

Aside from the "hard" sense of the chaotic there is the "soft," that notion of chaos as a revivifying challenge to oppressive or stultifying structures. It is a sense that is associated with health rather than illness. In James I have termed it *domesticated chaos*. What is its relationship to disorientation? In James this variety of the chaotic has to do with fluidity, vagueness, indeterminacy, multiplicity, and fragility, and, perhaps, we can associate these qualities generally with "soft" chaos. Clearly they are not limit categories; they do not describe something that is out of the bounds of human experience. So domesticated chaos is not paradoxical. It does not make possible the impossible. It is not an approximation of utter disorientation. Nonetheless, it is a relative disorientation. It tends to undermine the certainty of any particular orientation by dissolving its demarcations of identities, roles, definitions, and directions. Who we are, where we are, and where we are going become more shadowy matters, losing their keen outlines and their sharp forms.

This is a notion that seems important to postmodernist thinkers like Derrida, Foucault, Roland Barthes, and, on the religious side, Mark Taylor. In *Erring: A Postmodern A/theology*, Taylor observes that "individuals appear to be unsure of where they have come from and where they are going. Thus they are not certain where they are."[24] In a word, they are disoriented, though not, we should note, utterly disoriented. It is a group in which Taylor numbers himself and I should probably count myself, as well. Since it is a predicament common to the modern period, we can include Matthew Arnold who expressed it well when he said that we are "Wandering between two worlds, one dead, / The other powerless to be born."[25] The dead world is an oppressive one about which we cannot really use the past tense since we still mourn it and, like the dead father, it still dominates us. Four of its chief terms are *God*, *self*, *history*, and *book*. Taylor takes up deconstructive criticism in order to "dissolve" and disorganize the traditional structures whose lingering influence we need to escape. His "a/theology," then, is chaotic by being "never fixed but . . . always in transition." It is "irregular, eccentric, and vagrant"; "paradoxical, double, duplicitous, excentric, improper . . . errant."[26]

Taylor's a/theology is liminal; it dwells in the space between firm structures where forms have lost their shape. For Victor Turner, liminality is characterized by the ambiguous and indeterminate: "Liminal entities are neither here nor there; they are betwixt and between the positions assigned and arrayed by law, custom, convention, and ceremonial."[27] So liminality is associated with disorientation—who we are, where we are, and where we are bound are no longer established, but it is not a wrenching, disturbing disorientation. It is, in fact, a desirable one.[28] Taylor urges the "profitless play" that can come about when "individual identities dissolve and social oppositions break down."[29] Ritually, of course, the liminal period enables the transition from one identity to another and offers respite from the rigors of role and responsibility.

The liminal is chaotic but it is not threatening. It is, in fact, creative. Where definition is at a minimum, new, perhaps more authentic definition can arise. As N. J. Girardot points out, chaos is the primal soup from which comes creation, and thus it can refresh life if it is periodically embraced.[30] It is important to note that there is not utter disorientation in liminality: instead, terms like *confused*, *ambiguous*, *indistinct*, or *indeterminate* are used. Identities are inverted or they are multiple or, perhaps, they are confused, but they are not destroyed.

I stated in chapter 2 that chaos depends on contrast to something more structured, ordered, or formed. The difference between "hard" and "soft" chaos lies in the degree of violence in that contrast, one bursting boundaries and the other dissolving them. The other critical difference between them is in the attitude toward the disorder. Hard chaos is threatening and soft chaos not. Liminality in the deconstructive critics (or in ritual) does not seek to obliterate orientation or to point out the reality of the destruction of form and direction. It seeks to counteract such notions as finality, ultimacy, determinacy, security, permanence, totality, and mastery. It is a critical enterprise, not a constructive one. Yet a thinker like Taylor seems to want to weave such chaotic criticism into the fabric of orientation, through the reformulation of the four cardinal concepts of God, self, history, and book.[31] In this way, he is similar to James who depicted the dissolving, multiplying, changing power of the chaotic as such an important part of consciousness. Taylor, like James in the *Principles*, would seem to want to integrate the chaotic into orientation to create health, rather than using the chaotic to indicate the end of orientation and the fact of illness.

These two notions of the chaotic are beneficial in strongly contrasting ways, and consequently their religious values are quite different. Disruptive chaos gives us access to an experience not actually accessible to humans. It threatens the existence of any sort of orientation at all by insisting that, Lear-like, we sit naked on a heath while "cataracts and hurricanoes spout, . . . sulphurous and thought-executing fires . . . singe" our heads and "all-shaking thunder smite[s] flat the thick rotundity o' the world."[32] Without the power of such a symbol, we are more poorly oriented, living perhaps, in Chautauquas, "without a sin, without a victim, without a tear."[33] With such chaos, we have the orientations of angst and despair, the *mysterium tremendum* and the wrath of God, Job's torments, and the voice from the whirlwind. We are able to frame for ourselves the boundless terror of nuclear destruction and of the attempted extermination of whole peoples. We might say that we would be better off without much that "chaos" is able to present to us. Nonetheless, life demands the symbol of "hard" chaos, and religious orientations have been invaluable through time in part because they have made use of it.

"Soft" chaos has been of benefit religiously, as well. While it lacks the strength and power of disruptive chaos, while it does not present a limit notion like disorientation to us, it may be a more workable concept by lying much closer to mundane experience. Despair, angst, the wrath of God, and utter perplexity are all much closer to everyday life than we might often think. We don't have to probe very far to discover tragedy in any life, but it usually surfaces infrequently, while "soft" chaos is a useful category on a much more quotidian basis.

It has been a perennial religious theme that we are not at home on earth. We belong among the eternal forms, or in heaven, or in the Promised Land, and meanwhile we are imprisoned in physical forms, are tested, or wander in the diaspora. There are numerous varieties of the common religious notion that humans are estranged. The theme is visible in both romanticism and religious liberalism in the struggle against limitations to knowledge and experience and in the concern for the autonomy and integrity of the individual. In Blake's words, "the bounded is loathed by its possessor"; it is a "dull round." We can expand and escape through the exercise of passion, energy, or "Poetic Genius."[34] Schleiermacher chaffs at the notion that religious experience is uniform, static, or fixed, explaining that there are as many relationships to the Whole as there are individuals and that those relationships are constantly changing. Liberation, feminist, and black theology in the present day are alert to the injustice, confusion, and alienation that result when cultural categories made by others are forced to fit. As Blake put it in 1790, "One Law for the Lion & Ox is Oppression."[35]

Throughout these examples, strangeness and difference are the themes. It is here that "soft," dissolving chaos has been of religious use. Where concepts of human nature (to Blake), religious experience (to Schleiermacher), or religious symbols (to alternative theologies) have become disorienting and even dangerous by being too rigid or wrong, they need to be dissolved and reformed. Religious definition becomes indistinct in feeling or in passion. Experience is made authentic through multiplicity and differentiation. Oppressive symbols are rendered harmless and become the raw materials of new symbols if melted down. "Soft" chaos is a concept that makes such criticism and readjustment possible. It presents the possibility of dissolving structures, orders, and forms that have become inflexible, tired, or oppressive by countering them with fluidity, vagueness, indeterminacy, multiplicity, and fragility. It benefits religious orientation by disengaging us from beliefs that are no longer able to orient us adequately. In that way, soft chaos disorients us. Unlike "hard" chaos, it does not bring us close to utter disorientation. It simply makes existing orientations more fluid, more vague, or less clear.

"Ordinariness": the rhetoric of religious symbols

Clifford Geertz states that "religion tunes human actions to an envisaged cosmic order," and he notes that "we have very little idea of how, in empirical terms, this particular miracle is accomplished."[36] He is speaking, of course, of how we become oriented. This book has attempted to contribute to the understanding of the "miracle," though with a literary, not a sociological or anthropological, analysis.

So how do we become oriented? In lecture, sermon, and book we are told what shape the universe, life, and death have. In rituals of the ecclesiastical, political, or educational sorts, we enact our positions relative to others and the cosmos, and hence become oriented. As Geertz says, the tuning takes place "annually, weekly, daily, for some people almost hourly."[37] I believe that religion is a far more mundane matter than even that schedule implies. It does not rely on a once in a millennium prophet, a once in a lifetime conversion, a once a year celebration of Easter or Ramadan, or even a once a day prayer. If religion is orientation, it is among the most ordinary matters, as constant as vision, hearing, or smell. In fact, as often as we use cultural symbols that imply a particular shape to humans and the universe, we are oriented.

I believe that we can best see the *ordinariness* of religious "tuning" by turning briefly to the religious symbol. I am using symbol as Paul Tillich, Mircea Eliade, and Ernst Cassirer use it: as that which "opens up" or "unlocks" both reality and ourselves, though I would prefer Cassirer's emphasis on the formative rather than revelatory power of the symbol: it "produces and posits a world of its own."[38] It is the sacred symbol alone which, for Eliade, is able to "reveal [I'd prefer "create"] the fixed point, the central axis for all future orientation."[39] This book, then has been trying to make explicit the religious symbol, chaos, as it is variously evident in James's two works, particularly as it functions to "posit" a world (and self) through James's style.

Yet it is far too common to think of religious symbols as being rare, elevated, and somewhat transparent to their referent, to lose, that is, their ordinariness and the power of that ordinariness, and that is what I would like to emphasize here. What I mean by "ordinariness" is contained, I believe, in T. S. Eliot's quite astounding list of religiously significant aspects of British culture in *Notes Towards the Definition of Culture*. The elements of "our *lived* religion" include, he says, "Derby Day, Henley Regatta, Cowes, the twelfth of August, a cup final, the dog races, the pin table, the dart board, Wensleydale cheese, boiled cabbage cut into sections, beetroot in vinegar, nineteenth-century Gothic churches and the music of Elgar."[40] I believe it is the boiled cabbage that I appreciate most. Coming from a poet who had believed in the largely inaccessible nature of the religious (involving "a lifetime's death in love / Ardour and selflessness and self-surrender"), it is quite a list. I do not wish to make any claims about Eliot's own view of symbol. I simply wish to place his list on the page so we can observe (in spite of its many peculiarities) how ordinary many of these symbols are. He is not speaking of symbols that are elevated and rare: the eucharist, Palm Sunday, the surplice, and Westminster Abbey. He's speaking of boiled cabbage. This symbol (and several of the others) is absolutely plain, that is, not anything special, and yet, if it truly is a religious symbol, it must, in Geertz's phrase, "tune human actions to an envisaged cosmic order." That seems to be an astounding idea. Moreover, such a symbol does not occur "annually, weekly, daily, for some people almost hourly"; it occurs *constantly*. It is a *very* ordinary symbol.

It allows for the fact that religion is a completely mundane phenomenon. We are surrounded by religious symbols. In fact, we might say that *each* element of our surroundings may (and perhaps does) serve as a religious symbol, shaping our notions of ourselves and our world, orienting us. If I look at the sun, I am reminded, however subliminally, of the sun's cultural significance. I divide it from the earth; I set it in a firmament; I feel its power and my need. It is a late god, a stellar object, a thermonuclear source, a measure of the day and of seasons. All would seem to tune, that is, to orient me. Similarly, the smell of diesel through my window might carry suggestions of cancer or of Fernand Leger, recollections of wintry evenings in Istanbul, intimations of human power and of ecological responsibility. Apparently, any participation in cultural symbols, which is to say, any sight, smell, feeling, taste, sound or thought, can be religiously orienting.

Moreover, such ordinariness is undermined if it is implied that it is not the boiled cabbage that "tunes" us, but the divinity or the true nature of the universe that passes through to us by means of the cabbage. This is not the time to go into a full comparison of referential and nonreferential theories of religious symbol, but I would like to urge that it is important to preserve the formative ability of the ordinary object (action, word, sound, event, person, etc.). I am strongly reminded of Samuel Taylor Coleridge's agitated response to claims of the infallible inspiration of Scripture.

> Why should I not [believe infallibility]? Because the Doctrine in question petrifies at once the whole body of Holy Writ with all its harmonies and symmetrical gradations,—the flexile and the rigid,—the supporting hard and the clothing soft,—the blood

which is the life,—the intelligencing nerves, and the rudely
woven, but soft and springy, cellular substance, in which all are
embedded and lightly bound together. This breathing organ-
ism, the glorious *panharmonium*, which I had seen stand on
its feet as a man, and with a man's voice given to it, the Doc-
trine in question turns at once into a colossal Memnon's head,
a hollow passage for a voice, a voice that mocks the voices of
many men, and speaks in their names, and yet is but one voice
and the same;—and no man uttered it, and never in the human
heart was it conceived.[41]

Coleridge objects to what he calls "ventriloquism." and he
urges the integrity of the human voice. While I am not suggesting that his view of symbol is identical to that which I am
urging here, it is a similar integrity that I would like to preserve for all religious symbols: the notion that they are spoken *through* has quite different implications than that they
themselves speak.

It has been the presupposition of this study that as a religious symbol chaos is not transparent to the true nature of
the universe, and certainly not a vehicle for a divinity.
"Chaos" makes claims about the "shapeless" shape of the
world and of ourselves. It has a form and it forms us. It performs its work. Is it ordinary? I would say so. It's as plain as
any mess or muddle, and we encounter it as frequently as the
top of our desks, titles at the local bookstore, and all allusions
to (or introspections of) the "stream of consciousness."

This view of the ordinariness of religious symbol has two
implications for the relationship between religion and
rhetoric. First, *all* elements of culture have symbolic value; all
may form us religiously. That would include not only boiled
cabbage and diesel fumes, but certainly rhetoric, as well.
Rhetoric has a particular shape to it. This is evident, for
example, in Walter Beale's study where he presents the principles and norms of four kinds of discourse: scientific, instrumental, poetic, and rhetorical. Rhetoric has a characteristic
purpose, subject, author-audience relation, condition for success, occasion and context, and language and strategy. It
seeks to create and foster "consensus in communities." It
"deals in a world of probabilities and uncertainties. The solu-

tions it creates and the agreements and identifications that it fosters are temporary and fragile," requiring reinforcement. Rhetoric "arises out of and is already related to the immediate and long-range problems of communities." It functions to adjust "ideas to people and people to ideas." Finally, it moves "toward the common interests, the common capabilities, and the common norms and values of communities."[42] The particular form of rhetoric comes to shape those who participate in it, in a way that is distinct from the other forms of discourse. One who participates in (or is oriented by) rhetoric, then, is formed differently than one who participates in (and is oriented by) scientific discourse. It is much the same as it is with literary genres. The assumptions about the nature of the self, the nature of others, the relationship to the world and much else are vastly different in narrative, as opposed to lyric or drama. Each cultural form, then, be it rhetoric or scientific discourse, narrative or lyric, the business letter or the nursery rhyme may (and usually does) function as a religious symbol, forming selves and worlds.

In addition, and more largely, I have been assuming throughout this study that religion is strongly rhetorical. As Kenneth Burke notes, "rhetoric is the art of persuasion, and religious cosmogonies are designed, in the last analysis, as exceptionally thoroughgoing modes of persuasion."[43] James's writings, I have argued, attempt to persuade us to "front" life as they do. They shape us and our worlds in one of two chaotic forms. "Shaping," "forming," "orienting," and "tuning" are four of the principle metaphors I have used in this study for what it is that religions, symbols, and elements of culture (such as style) *do*. Though there are certainly vast differences between this constructivist, "world-making" view of religion and traditional rhetoric, it is useful to expand rhetoric to include these operations. James's *Varieties* and *Principles* attempt to *persuade* us, as do all symbols, all elements of culture.

One advantage of this emphasis on rhetoric is its implicitly communal basis. The rhetoric practiced by boiled cabbage (or by chaos or by rhetoric itself) is tied to a community from which it emerges, to which it is addressed, and whose particular problems are its concern. Rhetoric is language designed to do work—however largely that work may be conceived, for "orientation" can seem like very impractical work—and it must be subject to scrutiny and evaluation. If rhetoric is dangerous, if it does not move "toward the common interests . . . of communities," then the rhetoric can be changed. All of the elements of culture, which is to say, all of the elements of our surroundings, are engaged in profoundly powerful persuasion. It is certainly not all equally valuable. The persuasion accomplished by boiled cabbage (and it would be fascinating to speculate about what that may be) is not equivalent to that by prophets or conversions, marriage rites or mantras. All orienting, all religious symbols, all rhetoric is certainly not equally powerful, reverberating, or valuable. But I would urge that we not concentrate solely on the arduous, extraordinary, and rare, but examine, too, the very ordinary. And make sure our rhetoric serves our needs.

Notes

Introduction

1. LWJ, I, pp. 103-4.

2. Leon Edel, *Henry James: The Untried Years* (Philadelphia: Lippincott, 1953), p. 243.

3. Perry, p. 585.

4. *Ibid.*, p. 316.

5. Gerald E. Myers, *William James: His Life and Thought* (New Haven: Yale University Press, 1986), pp. 43-44, 317.

6. *Ibid.*, p. 668.

7. One exception is Charlene Haddock Seigfried's essay, "Vagueness and the Adequacy of Concepts," *Philosophy Today* 26 (Winter 1982), pp. 357-67. I would certainly agree with her when she states that "James's 'dramatic' rather than 'systematic' style was not the failing he (in less self-confident moments) and others often took it to be, but was a fitting match of content and expression" (p. 358).

8. VRE, p. 117; PP, I, p. 438.

9. ERE, p. 24 . The Dyak' s head is a favorite image to Richard R. Niebuhr who turned my attention to it as an apt figure for the chaotic in James. The editors of ERE point out that the Dyak's head appears frequently in James's unpublished papers. It seems appropriate that James should be so taken with the figure: it seems oddly parallel to his collection of photographs of writers and correspondents, though here, most explicitly, the universe has a chaotic face.

10. *Chaos* and the *chaotic* are awfully slippery terms, in great part because they signify that there is formlessness. Yet how can we gain a grasp of what seemingly eludes grasp by definition? Part of the task of the opening two chapters will be to develop a controlled definition of the chaotic, while the first three chapters will

argue that the chaotic pervades both the *Principles* and the *Varieties*.

11. In this work I will use style, form, and manner of writing more or less synonymously.

12. James Sully, *Mind* (old series), xvi (1891), p. 393.

Chapter 1

1. Jacques Barzun. *A Stroll with William James* (New York: Harper, 1983), pp. 34ff.

2. Gay Wilson Allen, *William James: A Biography* (New York: Viking, 1967), p. vii.

3. William James, Preface to the Italian edition of *The Principles of Psychology* in PP, III, p. 1483.

4. James Sully, *Mind* (old series), xvi (1891), P. 394.

5. PP, I, p. 55.

6. Barzun, p. 34.

7. PP, III, p. 1483.

8. PP, I, p. 15.

9. Josiah Royce, *William James and Other Essays on the Philosophy of Life* (New York: Macmillan, 1911), pp. 21-25; Vincent Burnelli, *Josiah Royce* (New York: Twayne, 1964), pp.73-74; Royce, *The Problem of Christianity* (New York: Macmillan, 1914), I, p. xvi.

10. Royce, *Problem of Christianity*, I, p. xvi.

11. See, for example, Richard Rorty, "Pragmatism, Relativism, and Irrationalism," in *The Consequences of Pragmatism* (Minneapolis: University of Minnesota Press, 1982), pp. 160-75.

12. William Dean, "Radical Empiricism and Religious Art," *Journal of Religion* 61, 2 (April 1981), pp. 169-71.

13. Louis J. Halle, *Out of Chaos* (Boston: Houghton, 1977), pp. 120, 93.

14. WB, p. 136.

15. Halle, p. 75.

16. *Ibid.*, pp. 545-46.

17. Sigmund Freud, *New Introductory Lectures on Psycho-analysis,* trans. W. J. H. Sprout (New York: Norton, 1933), p. 240; quoted in Barzun, p. 233.

18. Charlene Haddock Seigfried, *Chaos and Context: A Study in William James* (Athens: Ohio University Press, 1978). See especially pp. 1-53.

19. *Ibid.*, p. 28.

20. *Ibid.*, p. 32.

21. David M. LaGuardia, *Advance on Chaos: The Sanctifying Imagination of Wallace Stevens* (Hanover, N.H.: University Press of New England, 1983), p. 12.

22. *Ibid.*, p 19.

23. *Ibid.*, p. 26.

24. The four are formism, mechanism, contextualism, and organicism. Pepper says that James and Peirce began contextualism, of which he says "disorder is a categorical feature," yet contextualism is far larger in scope than the chaotic; the world hypothesis is more a metaphysic. Stephen C. Pepper, *World Hypotheses: A Study in Evidence* (Berkeley: University of California Press, 1942), p. 234; for contextualism see especially pp. 141-50, 232-79.

25. See Ninian Smart, *Worldviews: Crosscultural Explorations of Human Beliefs* (New York: Scribner, 1983), especially pp. 1-11.

26. Cf. Pepper, pp. 91-92.

27. See chapters 1, 2, 4, and 6 in Nelson Goodman, *Ways of Worldmaking* (Indianapolis: Hackett, 1978).

28. In fact, James's manner of writing may be sufficient to the creation of a chaotic world, independent of the "content" of his works. But, in any event, style and content (if I may use a dichotomy that this work attempts to undermine) seem to operate harmoniously in both the *Principles* and the *Varieties.*

29. I pair the two works first because the *Varieties* is sometimes considered a kind of third volume of the *Principles*, since it most explicitly picks up the concerns with psychology that James

had worked on from his illness in the 1870s until the completion of the massive text in 1890. For that reason alone it is natural to examine the two, but an even better reason is that these two works seem to contain so much of James the man, more even than his other works. This is, of course, a risky statement, for if what greatly interested James in his reading was the sense of a person behind a writing, he also managed to invest his own work with a strong presence. So while one could not say that James was absent from *Pragmatism* or from any of his collections of essays, such as *The Will to Believe*, one does have the sense that there is more of James in the *Principles* and the *Varieties*, and that in them we have a stronger sense of someone "fronting" life, perhaps because they deal with a topic as intimate as the life of the mind. Finally, I pair these works because in spite of their commonalities, they seem to depict the chaotic in very different ways. If the chaotic is a basic characterization of the world, we have, in the two works, different worlds.

30. *Oxford English Dictionary*, s.v. "chaos."

31. PP, I, p. 149.

32. PP, I, p. 277.

33. PP, I, p. 381.

34. The translation is John Dryden's from *Ovid's Metamorphoses in Fifteen Books*, translated by the most Eminent Hands (London: Jacob Tonsun, 1717), Bk. I, line 7 (p. 1).

35. Insisture is regularity.

36. *The Tragedy of Troilus and Cressida*, act I, sc. iii, lines 83-126.

37. Blaise Pascal, *Pensees* (New York: Dutton, 1958), #434, p. 121.

38. This is true both of the cosmological and figurative uses of chaos. In cosmology, chaos is absence of cosmos, but it is also a swirling cloud of elements or Ovid's rough undigested mass.

39. James says it himself in *Pragmatism*. "A 'chaos,' once so named, has as much unity of discourse as a cosmos." What must be decided is whether there can be a chaos without naming one. James vacillates on this, as we shall see. James, *Pragmatism*, p. 66.

40. Kant deals with chaos in the Third Critique. We feel the sublime when our shaping powers are frustrated by the formless in nature. "In what we are accustomed to call sublime there is nothing at all that leads to particular objective principles and forms of nature corresponding to them; so far from it that, for the most part, nature excites the ideas of the sublime in its chaos or in its wildest and most irregular disorder and desolation." (*Critique of Judgment*, transl. J. H. Bernard (New York: Hafner Press, 1951), section 23, p. 84). What we perceive is "boundlessness"; that is, the "formless object" is figured to our experience by the concept of boundlessness (p. 82). Yet such a perception is felt as unsatisfactory since it seems "to violate purpose in respect of the judgment, to be unsuited to our presentational faculty, and as it were to do violence to the imagination" (p. 83). It may be for this reason that Kant says that what is involved in the sublime is not the concepts of the understanding but the ideas of reason, that is, the ideas that unify experience. The sublime—the chaotic—seems to violate the possibility of experience itself. Perceiving it as "boundlessness" frustrates us very basically, "checking the vital powers." But such a perception also causes "a consequent stronger outflow" of those vital powers and causes us to reflect on and respect our own "destination" of being adequate to the comprehension of the whole" (section 27, p. 96). That is, the ideas of reason require our comprehension of the whole, unfrustrated by any purposelessness or boundlessness. Since they ask it, it must be possible. So its frustration by the chaotic only causes us to be more aware of and respect more highly that requirement and destiny.

41. Ernst Cassirer, *Language and Myth*, transl. Suzanne K. Langer (New York: Dover, 1946), p. 8.

42. Gordon D. Kaufman, *An Essay on Theological Method*, rev. ed. (Missoula, Mont.: Scholar's Press, 1979), p. 5. The argument I have been tracing would not be uncongenial to James himself, who argues for the figured nature of all perception: when a sensation could be interpreted in more than one way, he says, we do not mix them and get a blur. Our perceptions have one definite form or another. Such a notion need only be added to James's commitment to the role of interest in perception and thought—it is our forms that determine thought and perception, not forms "already there"—to have a position close to that of Kaufman. See PP, p. 728.

43. *The Tragedy of Othello*, act III, sc. iii, lines 90-92.

44. Thomas Hobbes, *Leviathan: or the Matter. Form and Power of a Commonwealth. Ecclesiasticall or Civill*, ed. A. R.Weller (Cambridge: Cambridge University Press, 1935), Bk. III, section xxxvi, p. 232.

45. Kate Chopin, *The Awakening* (New York: Garrett Press, 1970), p. 34.

46. Wallace Stevens, *Collected Poems* (New York: Knopf, 1976), p. 70.

47. *Ibid*.

48. Henry Adams, *The Education of Henry Adams* (Boston: Houghton, 1918), chapter 13.

49. PP, I, pp. 224-30.

50. PP, I, p. 754.

51. PU, p. 39; WB, p. 118.

52. Thomas R. Martland, *The Metaphysics of William James and John Dewey: Process and-Structure in Philosophy and Religion* (New York: Philosophical; Library, 1963), p. 49; see especially chapter 2.

53. Barnard P. Brennan, *William James* (New York: Twayne, 1968), pp. 126-37. Stuart Hampshire describes James's vision as of a "Heraclitean flux." Stuart Hampshire, "Amiable Genius," Review of *William James: Writings 1902-1910*, ed. Bruce Kuklick. *New York Review of Books*, XXXV, 9 (1988), p. 17.

54. Gerald E. Myers, "Introduction: The Intellectual Context," in PP, I, p. xviii.

55. Henry James, *A Small Boy and Others* (New York: Scribner, 1913), p. 216.

56. Leon Edel, *Henry James: The Untried Years* (Philadelphia: Lippincott, 1953), p. 109; Henry James, Jr., Introduction to LWJ, p. 21.

57. *Ibid.*, p. 22.

58. Perry, I, p. 129.

59. *Ibid.*, p. 323.

60. *Ibid.*, p. 324.

61. Barzun, p. 17. Myers agrees, stating that James's reading of Renouvier "was not the only time that philosophizing helped James out of a depression; in fact, he continuously fought his emotional battles with thoughts and words, with philosophy." While Myers feels that philosophy could help cure James, he believes that the cause of his problems could have been either "too intense a moral and religious upbringing result[ing] in an overpowering superego" or purely physiological causes. *William James: His Life and Thought* (New Haven: Yale University Press, 1986), pp. 47, 21. See especially pp. 15-53.

62. Allen, pp. xii, 149, 163.

63. Howard M. Feinstein, *Becoming William James* (Ithaca: Cornell University Press, 1984), pp. 298-329.

64. James William Anderson, *"William James' Depressive Period (1867-1872) and the Origins of his Creativity,"* Ph.D. diss., University of Chicago, 1980.

65. Perry, I, p. 293.

66. VRE, p. 134.

67. LWJ, p. 100.

68. *Ibid.*, p. 75.

69. *Ibid.*, p. 148.

70. *Ibid.*, p. 96.

71. Perry, I, p. 287.

72. WB, p. 62. James's desire for inclusiveness takes a different form in this period than later. In these crisis years when it is the universe that possesses all gravitational force, we see James wanting to flow into all; later, once James acquires his own mass, he will seek inclusion by taking all within. Hence, it is participation, which he seeks early on and inclusiveness later. In both cases, the basic impulse seems very similar.

73. LWJ, p. 148.

74. Perry, I, p. 301.

75. *Ibid.*, p. 309.

76. *Ibid.*, p. 301.

77. EP, p. 4.

78. *Ibid.*

79. Perry, I, p. 343.

Chapter 2

1. PP, I, p. 219.

2. The relevance of James's view of neurology to the chaotic will be discussed later in this chapter.

3. PP, II, p. 1232n. He makes similar statements in PP, I, p. 381, and PP, II, p. 1231.

4. *Ibid.*

5. PP, I, p. 277.

6. PP, II, p. 1231.

7. *Ibid.*, pp. 1231, 959.

8. Significantly enough, James does not indicate how we are able to select from this soup, a problem that may be solved by his hypothesis of pure experience in his later work.

9. PP, I, p. 277.

10. *Ibid.*, p. 273.

11. PP, II, p. 1232n.

12. *Ibid.*, p. 1231n.

13. PP, I, pp. 434-35.

14. PP, II, p. 1232n.

15. *Ibid.*, p. 1229.

16. Voltaire, "Well, Everything Is Well," transl. Robert M. Adams, in *Candide or Optimism* (New York: Norton, 1966), pp. 86-91.

17. In "Is Life Worth Living" James discusses whether we can usefully speak of what we don't know, concluding that we must trust to "maybes." Yet in his discussion there is in the context of the question of suicide where our "vital interest" is involved in such

a "maybe." It is somewhat questionable whether the shape of reality prior to our experience is of vital interest, at least in the *Principles*. WB, pp. 48-56.

18. Charlene Haddock Seigfried, *Chaos and Context: A Study in William James* (Athens: Ohio University Press, 1978), pp. 1-53.

19. Tom D. Driver, "Beckett by the Madeleine," *Columbia University Forum* IV, 3 (Summer 1961), pp. 21-23. The interview was only later written down by Driver who reports that it is very close to Beckett's own words.

20. *Ibid.*, p. 22.

21. David H . Hesla, *The Shape of Chaos: An Interpretation of the Art of Samuel Beckett* (Minneapolis: University of Minnesota Press, 1971), pp. 7, 8.

22. Raymond Federman, *Journey to Chaos: Samuel Beckett's Early Fiction* (Berkeley: University of California Press, 1965), pp. 4, 9.

23. It has also been used in discussions of Joseph Heller and more broadly cultural analyses of economics and ecology. On Heller see Lindsey Tucker, "Entropy and Information Theory in Heller's *Something Happened*," *Contemporary Literature* 25, 3 (Fall 1984). On culture see Jeremy Rifkin and Ted Howard, *Entropy: A New World View* (New York: Viking, 1980).

24. Peter L. Abernethy, "Entropy in Pynchon's *The Crying of Lot 49*," *Critique* 14, 2 (1972), p. 20.

25. I owe this formulation to Richard R. Niebuhr. This notion of chaos is similar to Mircea Eliade's characterization of profane space—or chaotic space, as he often describes it—as homogeneous. There are simply no differences in profane space; it is "neutral"; there are no "breaks." Sacred space, on the other hand, is heterogeneous. The sacred gives a "fixed point" that orders the world. See *The Sacred and the Profane* (New York: Harcourt, 1959), pp. 20-24.

26. I am indebted to Gordon Kaufman for this observation.

27. James Gleick, *Chaos: Making a New Science* (New York: Viking, 1987), pp. 3, 39-43.

28. The two realms are analogous but are not identical, in spite

of Seigfried who lumps characteristics of consciousness with those
of "outer reality" as both comprising the "chaotic." Lisa Ruddick,
too, confuses the stream of consciousness with the "unmediated"
world outside the mind. Seigfried, pp. 27-28; Ruddick, "Fluid Symbols in American Modernism: William James, Gertrude Stein,
George Santayana, and Wallace Stevens," in *Allegory, Myth, and
Symbol: Harvard English Studies*, ed. Morton W. Bloomfield (Cambridge: Harvard University Press, 1981), p. 338.

29. PP, I, pp. 219, 273.

30. PP, I, p. 220.

31. *Ibid.*, p. 233.

32. *Ibid.*, p. 234.

33. *Ibid.*, p. 238.

34. Richard R. Niebuhr expresses the aptness of the flight
metaphor unusually well. He notes that flight

> reveals[s] consciousness as being in significant measure a flow of feel-
> ings—a flow that is often swift or even headlong—connecting the
> "perchings" or larger objects of our thinking, that is, our images or
> ideas. . . . Our most intimate sense of self lies in mental activities, swift
> as flight, which we can scarcely arrest long enough to contemplate.

Niebuhr, "William James' Metaphysics of Religious Experience" in
*Streams of Grace: Studies of Jonathan Edwards, Samuel Taylor
Coleridge, and William James, The Neesima Lectures* (Kyoto,
Japan: Doshisha University Press, 1983), pp. 93-94.

35. PP, I., p. 246.

36. *Ibid.*, pp. 240ff, 250ff.

37. *Ibid.*, pp. 651-53.

38. *Ibid.*, pp. 610-12.

39. *Ibid.*, p. 533.

40. PP, I, p. 238.

41. PP, I, p. 246.

42. *Ibid.*, pp. 236, 244.

43. *Ibid* , pp. 236-37.

44. *Ibid.*, p. 543.

45. *Talks*, pp. 111-13. *Talks* collects a series of lectures James delivered in 1892 to Cambridge elementary and secondary school teachers on the usefulness of psychological insights for education. If the shorter version of the *Principles* eliminates "all polemics and history, all bibliography and experimental details, all metaphysical subtleties and digressions, all quotations, all humor and pathos, all *interest* in short," *Talks* pares matters down still further, offering a two- or three-page condensation of many of the chapters of the *Principles*. It is valuable for its very straightforward presentations of many of the topics in the *Principles*, and for its practical orientation. LWJ, I, p. 314.

46. PP, I, p. 34-35.

47. *Ibid.*, p. 227.

48. *Ibid.*, p. 224.

49. *Ibid.*, pp. 224-25.

50. PP, II, p. 1232n.

51. *Ibid.*, p. 1231.

52. PP, I, p. 219.

53. *Ibid.*, p. 394.

54. *Ibid.*, p. 281.

55. LWJ, I, p. 89.

56. WB, p. 77. *Pragmatism*, in particular, voices this view in its division of philosophies into the tough and tender-minded. See *Pragmatism*, pp. 11-14.

57. PP, I, p. 220.

58. *Ibid.*, p. 221.

59. *Ibid.*, pp. 222, 223.

60. *Ibid.*, p. 318.

61. *Ibid.*, p. 279, emphasis omitted.

62. *Ibid.*, p. 282.

63. *Ibid.*, p. 285.

64. *Ibid.*, p. 295.

65. *Ibid.*, p. 298.

66. *Ibid.*, p. 299. It is interesting to note that James uses this same quotation in the *Varieties* to exemplify healthy-mindedness. It indicates that the *Principles* is a work of health, as I will discuss later.

67. *Ibid.*, p. 273.

68. *Ibid.*, p. 274.

69. *Ibid.* It is not clear if James is actually distinguishing attention from sensation since he sees both creating differences out of what would be "a grey chaotic indiscriminateness" (p. 381). He seems to feel that we must always attend in order to sense. But elsewhere James seems to place attention subsequent to sensation, as in the discussion that follows.

70. *Ibid.*, pp. 394-95.

71. PP, II, p. 959; PP, I, p. 274.

72. *Ibid.*, p. 436.

73. *Ibid.*, pp. 434-435.

74. *Ibid.*, p. 400.

75. *Ibid.*, p. 397.

76. *Ibid.*, p. 400.

77. PP, II, p. 966.

78. *Ibid.*, p. 970.

79. *Ibid.*, p. 972.

80. Perry, I, p. 322.

81. PP, I, p. 262.

82. *Ibid.*, pp. 263-64.

83. *Ibid.*, p. 381.

84. *Ibid.*, p. 266.

85. Novalis, *Schriften* (Leipzig: Bibliographisches Institut U.G., n.d.), III, p. 43.

86. PP, I, p. 117.

87. *Ibid.*, p. 118.

88. *Ibid.*, p. 119.

89. *Ibid.*, p. 110.

90. *Ibid.*, p. 119.

91. PP, II, pp. 1186-87.

92. *Paradise Lost*, Bk. II, lines 891-97.

93. See *Metamorphoses*, Bk. I, lines 2-10, and *Paradise Lost*, Bk. II, lines 890-1055. "Rough, unordered mass" is Frank Justus Miller's translation (Cambridge: Harvard University Press, 1977).

94. For other antecedents in this tradition, see Merritt Y. Hughes, Introduction to *Paradise Lost,* in *John Milton: Complete Poems and Major Prose* ed. Hughes (New York: Odyssey Press, 1957), pp. 179-80.

95. *Paradise Lost*, II, lines 915-16 (p. 253).

96. *Metamorphoses*, Bk. I, lines 9-26; the translation is by Rolfe Humphries (Bloomington: Indiana University Press, 1957), p. 4.

97. James's sense of such a universe is similar to what Peter L. Thorslev, Jr. describes as the "open universe," a concept of a place that is neither nurturing nor threatening but humanly indifferent, where humans are forced to make their own destiny and can appeal to no absolutes of order. What I have termed the productivity of James's plenum consists only in its potential, in the fact that it is a raw material from which humans make their world. In Thorslev's sense it is "open," since it does not dictate what it will become. The same is true of good and evil in James's concept of the universe. "Visible nature is all plasticity and indifference—a moral multiverse, as one might call it, and not a moral universe" (WB, pp. 43-44). See Thorslev, *Romantic Contraries: Freedom and Destiny* (New Haven: Yale University Press, 1984), chapter 6, pp. 142-86, especially pp. 142-44.

98. PP, II, p. 754.

99. PP, I, p. 225.

100. *Ibid.*, p. 234.

101. *Ibid.*, p. 21.

102. *Talks*, 97-100.

103. Michael Riffaterre, *Text Production*, transl. Terese Lyons (New York: Columbia University Press, 1983), p. 5.

Chapter 3

1. Chautauqua was, in Gay Wilson Allen's words, "a combined summer resort and popular educational institution, where earnest people swam, boated, picnicked, and attended lectures." *William James: A Biography* (New York: Viking, 1967), p. 384.

2. *Talks*, p. 152.

3. *Ibid.*, pp. 152-53.

4. VRE, p. 154.

5. Perry, II, p. 677.

6. VRE, p. 153.

7. LWJ, I, p. 293.

8. VRE, p. 528.

9. LWJ, II, p. 127.

10. *Ibid.*, p. 77.

11. *Ibid.*, p. 78.

12. Allen, p. 388.

13. LWJ, II, pp. 66-67. See pp. 66-72, including Henry James Jr.'s summary of the affair.

14. Jacques Barzun, *A Stroll with William James* (New York: Harper, 1983), p. 170n. See Allen, p. 389.

15. VRE, p. 529.

16. *Ibid.*, p. 537.

17. Allen, p. 416.

18. *Ibid.*, p. 405.

19. VRE, p. 541.

20. LWJ, II, p. 96.

21. *Ibid.*, pp. 158, 161.

22. *Ibid.*, pp. 96, 158.

23. *Ibid.*, pp. 76-77.

24. Johann Wolfgang von Goethe, *Faust*, transl. Louis Mac-Neice (New York: Oxford University Press, 1951), p. 134.

25. Quoted in Roderick Nash, *Wilderness and the American Mind* (New Haven: Yale University Press, 1967), p. 128.

26. See Nash, especially chapter 9.

27. VRE, p. 137.

28. Quoted in Douglas Bush, *Matthew Arnold: A Survey of His Poetry and Prose* (New York: Macmillan, 1971), p. 40n.

29. LWJ, II, p. 248.

30. VRE, pp. 116, 117, 118.

31. *Ibid.*, p. 126.

32. See PP, II, pp. 1231-32.

33. *Ibid.*, p. 128.

34. *Ibid.*, p. 119.

35. *Ibid.*, p. 128.

36. *Ibid.*, pp. 139, 142, 143. James reverses the order in half of these instances. Spiritual, higher, useful, and ideal line up on one side and natural, lower, erring, and actual on the other.

37. This is where the two versions of evil meet: evil may be a basic reality or it may be the absence of creative interest: in either case what is needed is "a stimulus, an excitement, a faith, a force that re-infuses the positive willingness to live" (*Ibid.*, p. 156). The force seems analogous to the spiritual self he spoke of in the *Principles*; it is the aspect of self that drives interest, and thus creates both world and self. Evil as positive or as privative stimulates or requires the invigoration of that centripetal force of the self.

38. *Ibid.*, p. 143.

39. *Ibid.*, pp. 141, 146-47.

40. Or while evil is the undermining of the very process of making sense of the world by being the absence of the world-creating power of interest.

41. James mentions work by Myers, Binet, Janet, Breuer, Freud, Mason, and Prince as having contributed to his understanding of the subliminal self. VRE, pp. 190-91.

42. *Ibid.*, p. 170-71.

43. *Ibid.*, p. 168-69.

44. *Ibid.*, p. 95.

45. *Ibid.*, p. 174.

46. *Ibid.*, p. 177.

47. It might be important to repeat that it isn't the degree of violence that makes the chaotic, it's relative disorder. The smoothest stream may seem chaotic if compared with a well-delineated object, say a cube. Where are the edges of that piece of stream? And where is that piece of stream now?

48. See VRE., p. 146.

49. *Ibid.*, pp. 142, 154.

50. *Ibid.*, p. 201.

51. *Ibid.*, p. 294.

52. *Ibid.*, p. 407.

53. *Ibid.*, p. 234.

54. *Ibid.*, p. 238.

55. *Ibid.*, p. 279.

56. Perry, I, p. 322.

57. PP, I, p. 298.

58. See p. 38, this work..

59. *The Diary of Alice James,* ed. Leon Edel (New York: Penguin, 1982), December 14, 1889, pp. 67-68. His sister added, "His brain isn't limited to 14, perhaps unfortunately." One is reminded of Henry James's statement that "the house of fiction has not one window but a million." The James family was inclined toward mul-

tiplicity. Henry James, Preface to the New York edition, *Portrait of a Lady,* ed. Robert D. Bamberg (New York: Norton, 1975), p. 7.

60. VRE, pp. 104, 94, 104 .

61. *Ibid.*, p. 338.

62. *Ibid.*, p. 339.

63. *Ibid.*, p. 538. "Absurd," of course, means something considerably different to James and his contemporaries than it does to those living after Sartre, Beckett, and Camus.

64. *Ibid.*, p. 343.

65. *Ibid.*, p. 393.

66. *Ibid.*, p. 245.

67. *Ibid.*, p. 270.

68. *Ibid.*, p. 287.

69. *Ibid.*, p. 268.

70. *Ibid.*, pp. 387-88.

71. PP, I, pp. 273, 21.

72. VRE, p. 407.

73. *Ibid.*, p. 399. James actually quotes James Henry Leuba on this, but it is clearly a statement with which he strongly agrees.

74. *Ibid.*, p. 397.

75. *Ibid.*, p. 413.

76. *Ibid.*, p. 156.

Chapter 4

1. As Freud puts it in his *Autobiographical Study*, he and James were on a walk during Freud's first trip to America. James "stopped suddenly, handed me a bag he was carrying, and asked me to walk on, saying that he would catch me up as soon as he had got through an attack of angina pectoris which was just coming on. He died of that disease a year later; and I have always wished that I might be as fearless as he was in the face of approaching death." Freud, *An Autobiographical Study*, transl. James Strachey (London:

Hogarth Press, 1935), pp. 94-95. Freud calls pragmatism anarchy in his *New Introductory Lectures on Psychoanalysis*, transl. W. J. H. Sprout (New York: Norton, 1933), p. 240. Jones makes the comment about James's style in *The Life and Work of Sigmund Freud* (New York: Basic, 1953-57), II, p. 210. Gerald Myers notes a similar comparison by Rebecca West. She observes that "one [of the brothers] grew up to write fiction as though it were philosophy and the other to write philosophy as though it were fiction." West, *Henry James* (New York: Holt, 1916), p. 11; Myers, p. 21.

2. So Rousseau's style is crucial to Derrida, Nietzsche's to Alexander Nehamas (as well as Derrida) and Kierkegaard's to Louis Mackey. See Jacques Derrida, *Of Gramatology*, transl. Gayatri Chakrovorty Spivak (Baltimore: Johns Hopkins University Press, 1976); Alexander Nehamas, *Nietzsche: Life as Literature* (Cambridge: Harvard University Press, 1985); Louis Mackey, *Kierkegaard: A Kind of Poet* (Philadelphia: University of Pennsylvania Press, 1971). See Nehamas's first chapter especially in which he argues that Nietzsche's use of a multiplicity of styles is essential to presenting his perspectivism.

3. Goodman discusses worldmaking extensively and explicitly in *Ways of Worldmaking* (Indianapolis, Indiana: Hackett Publishing, 1978), and Goodman, *Of Minds and Other Matters* (Cambridge: Harvard University Press, 1984). He discusses it implicitly in *Languages of Art: An Approach to a Theory of Symbols* (Indianapolis: Hackett Publishing, 1976).

4. Stephen Crites, "The Narrative Quality of Experience," *Journal of the American Academy of Religion* 39, 3 (1971), p. 291.

5. Crites, pp. 300, 299, 302, 303, 306.

6. In a later article, Crites tries to edge away from this view of the unique mimesis of narrative. He does not mean to claim, he says, "that this convergence of art and experience occurs in narrative form alone. I am in general inclined to think that enduring esthetic forms and genre have their correlates and indeed their psychic sources in our most basic forms of experience." But he also says that "our common *Lebenswelt* contains what we encounter in immediate experience and deal with in our practical activity, to which narrative locution is our most direct linguistic access." In spite of his pluralistic instincts, Crites cannot get away from the

preeminence of narrative, which is due to its metaphysical truth. Crites, "Angels We Have Heard," in *Religion as Story*, ed. James B. Wiggins (New York: Harper, 1975), pp. 57n, 31.

7. Ted Estess, "The Inenarrable Contraption: Reflections on the Metaphor of Story," *Journal of the American Academy of Religions*, 42, 3 (1974), pp. 415-434.

8. Theologically fanaticism is taken to be the result of assuming we have gained access to that which is not in our reach (either not now or not ever). Paul Tillich identifies it with the demonic, that is, with "elevating something finite and transitory to infinite and eternal validity." H. Richard Niebuhr's "henotheism" is similar in choosing as the object of devotion something that is merely one among many. Gordon Kaufman points out the epistemological dimension of such theological thought by emphasizing the procedural error that results in idolatry: the assumption that we can penetrate to divine truth without cultural tools. That is a position that Stephen C. Pepper argues more generally, defining a dogmatist as "one whose belief exceeds his cognitive grounds for belief." Tillich, *Systematic Theology*, I (Chicago: University of Chicago Press, 1951), p. 3; Niebuhr, *Radical Monotheism and Western Culture* (New York: Harper, 1943); Kaufman, *The Theological Imagination: Constructing the Concept of God* (Philadelphia: Westminster Press, 1981); Pepper, *World Hypotheses: A Study in Evidence* (Berkeley: University of California Press, 1957), chapter 2.

9. Gerard Genette, "Frontiers of Narrative," in *Figures of Literary Discourse* (New York: Columbia University Press, 1982), p. 127.

10. Coleridge is not far different in his famous distinction between an imitation and a copy. The imitation depends on difference from an original whereas the (inferior) copy is based upon similarity. See Samuel Taylor Coleridge, "On Poesy or Art," in *Biographia Literaria*, ed. J. Shawcross (London: Oxford University Press, 1907), II, pp. 255-56. There is a very useful discussion of Coleridge's distinction in the edition of the *Biographia* by James Engell and W. Jackson Bate in *The Collected Works of Samuel Taylor Coleridge* (Princeton: Princeton University Press, 1983), I, pp. cv-cvi; II, p. 72, n4.

11. Genette, *Narrative Discourse: An Essay in Method* transl. Jane E. Lewin (Ithaca: Cornell University Press, 1980), p. 164.

12. Goodman, *Languages of Art: An Approach to a Theory of Symbols* (Indianapolis: Hackett Publishing, 1976), p. 31. See Goodman's entire discussion of "Reality Remade," pp. 3-43, which includes a consideration of imitation in chapter 1.

13. Tzvetan Todorov argues similarly that there is no "primitive" narrative. "No narrative is natural; a choice and a construction will always preside over its appearance; narrative is a discourse, not a series of events." The notion of verisimilitude as a faithfulness to events is mistaken, he claims. Todorov, "Primitive Discourse," in *The Poetics of Prose* transl. Richard Howard (Ithaca: Cornell University Press, 1977), p. 55.

14. Todorov, "An Introduction to Verisimilitude" in *Poetics*, pp. 80-88.

15. Roland Barthes, "Introduction to the Structural Analysis of Narratives," in *Image—Music—Text*, transl. Stephen Heath (New York: Hill and Wang, 1977), pp. 123-24.

16. Though form or genre alone would *tend* to create a particular order for readers, such shaping interacts with what is written in a particular work. That is, there is much room within the outlines of narrative and a particular work can add specifics, reinforce some aspects, and even efface others. It can also contradict, creating a reading experience of considerable tension. But considered by itself, the form of a work does a great deal of worldmaking.

17. Alastair Fowler, *Kinds of Literature: An Introduction to the Theory of Genres and Modes* (Cambridge: Harvard University Press, 1982), p. 236.

18. Some might suggest formlessness could be produced by a computer generating random letters, but, of course, that isn't really formless, either, for it would still be "random letters."

19. *Talks*, p. 62.

20. *Ibid.*, p. 62.

21. *Ibid.*, p. 63.

22. *Ibid.*, p. 69.

23. *Ibid.*, p. 64.

24. *Ibid.*, p. 69.

25. *Ibid.*, p. 68; italics omitted.

26. LWJ, I, p. 89.

27. LWJ, I, p. 296; Perry, II, p. 47.

28. *The Nation* LIII (1891), p. 33.

29. Fowler, chapter 4, pp. 54-74 .

30. PP, III, p. 1300; and these two thousand are only those cited: they do not include indirect quotations or references without notes.

31. PP, I, p. 62.

32. *Ibid.*, p. 55.

33. PP, II, p. 662.

34. PP, I, p. 119.

35. *Ibid.*, p. 199.

36. *Ibid* ., p. 205.

37. *Ibid.*, p. 125.

38. *Ibid.*, p. 192.

39. *Ibid.*, p. 398.

40. *Ibid.*, p. 537.

41. *Ibid.*, p. 293.

42. *Ibid.*, p. 281. Another vision is also on p. 281, this one imagining the loss of the social self.

43. *Ibid.*, p. 285, emphasis omitted.

44. *Ibid.*, p. 286.

45. *Ibid.*, pp. 286-87.

46. Frances de Sales, *Treatise on the Love of God* (1616), quoted in Louis L. Martz, *The Poetry of Meditation: A Study of English Religious Literature of the Seventeenth Century* (New Haven: Yale University Press, 1954), p. 15.

47. PP, I, p. 124.

48. *Ibid.*, pp. 130-31.

49. In *Pragmatism* James makes a point that echoes this multiplicity of forms. One monistic view, he says, is that the world is an aesthetic union, that "things tell a story. Their parts hang together so as to work out a climax." James prefers the pluralistic view. "The world is full of partial stories that run parallel to one another, beginning and ending at odd times. They mutually interlace and interfere at points, but we cannot unify them completely in our minds." *Pragmatism*, pp. 70-71.

50. *Ibid.*, p. 238.

51. Charlene Haddock Seigfried takes a similar position in her essay. "James found the multi-faceted aspects of experience more clearly communicated in terms which were themselves multi-leveled." Seigfried, "Vagueness and the Inadequacy of Concepts," *Philosophy Today* 26 (Winter), p. 362.

52. Barbara K. Lewalski, *Paradise Lost and The Rhetoric of Literary Forms* (Princeton: Princeton University Press, 1985). See especially chapter 1.

53. Mikhail Bakhtin, *The Dialogic Imagination*, ed. Michael Holquist, transl. Caryl Emerson and Michael Holquist (Austin: University of Texas Press, 1981), pp. 320-21.

54. *Ibid.*, p. 265.

55. *Ibid.*, pp. 270-72.

56. Wayne C. Booth, Introduction to *Problems of Dostoevsky's Poetics,* ed. and transl. Caryl Emerson (Minneapolis: University of Minnesota Press, 1984), p. xxi.

57. PP, I, pp. 295-99 .

58. One would assume that to be Goethe.

59. Wolfgang Iser, *The Act of Reading: A Theory of Aesthetic Response* (Baltimore: Johns Hopkins Press, 1978), pp. 118-34.

60. *Ibid.*, p. 126.

61. Cf. *ibid.*, pp. 183-85.

62. *Ibid.*, p. 184.

63. *Ibid.*, pp. 184-85.

64. Jerome Bruner calls this process "subjunctivizing reality."

One characteristic of the narrative as opposed to the paradigmatic or scientific mode, he says, is to "traffic in possibilities not certainties." Bruner, *Actual Minds. Possible Worlds* (Cambridge: Harvard University Press, 1986), pp. 25-26.

65. PP, I, pp. 117-26. Of the chapter on habit I omit only the opening four paragraph introduction and the concluding "How To" guide on making habits an ally, which finishes with the exhortation considered earlier.

66. James does come through as a somewhat eccentric person, though certainly one for whom a reader feels affection. One illustration that shows James's somewhat endearing oddness comes in his chapter on "The Perception of 'Things.'" James writes of the distorted perception that results "if we lie on the floor and look up at the mouth of the person talking behind us." It seems an effective demonstration, but to know that it works James must have tried it, and that gives us an amusing picture of James, indeed. See PP, II, p. 727.

67. *Ibid.*, pp. 953, 956, 957.

68. *Ibid.*, pp. 740-41.

69. I do not believe that we gain an unalloyed view of an author through a text: the voice in James's pages is, of course, a created voice, not a voice directly heard. But we can construct a self from its many selves, and that is an interesting task not only for psychology but for those concerned with books, as well. Michael Riffaterre argues that the uniqueness of each text means that we cannot put together a composite view of the author of a corpus. I believe that such composition produces useful consequences, among them the realization that such multiplicity can be the expression of single human beings. Riffaterre, *Text Production,* transl. Terese Lyons (New York: Columbia University Press, 1983). See esp. chapter 1.

I should note here that James does not limit his personalizing to himself. Thoughts of the same ego recognize one another "as blood-relatives"; a river thinks, "I am here flowing . . . in the direction of greatest resistance. . . ."; and, one of the finest examples, a polyp is able to conceive "if a feeling of 'Hollo! thinkumbob again!' ever flitted through its mind." PP, I, pp. 314, 427, 438.

70. *Talks*, p. 69.

71. PP, I, pp. 121-22. James, Carpenter, and, particularly, the editors of the Harvard University Press edition of the *Principles,* are all unclear about the source of this quotation. It is said to be a translation of Houdin's autobiography, *Confidences d'un prestidigiteur,* yet Houdin speaks in only a portion of the passage. There is no indication whose the other voice is.

72. PP, I, p. 125.

73. Michael Holquist, Introduction in Bakhtin, *Dialogic Imagination,* p. xxix.

74. See pp. 60-62 this work.

75. See p. 60 this work.

76. PP, II, p. 740; PP, I, pp. 224-25, 394.

77. Lawrence Buell, *Literary Transcendentalism: Style and Vision in the American Renaissance* (Ithaca: Cornell University Press, 1973), p. 170. See chapter 6, "Catalogue Rhetoric," pp. 166-87.

78. *Pragmatism*, p. 73. See Lecture IV, "The One and the Many" in *Pragmatism*, pp. 63-79.

79. PP, II, p. 1232n.

80. Buell, pp. 170, 174. Buell's concern is to rescue the enumerative catalog from accusations of anarchy, and he does so by pointing out the coherence that exists within the lists. He concludes that they are microcosms "of a fluid but cohesive universe." To my mind, of course, that does not exclude these catalogs from being chaotic, just from being of the "utter disorder and confusion" sort of chaos. Having some sort of coherence does not exclude chaos, as I hope I've made clear. Nonetheless, the patterns of relationship that Buell finds in the catalogs of Emerson and Whitman agree with my argument that James's lists have more in common with domesticated than disruptive chaos.

81. The statement is made with literal emphasis: James places it in italics . PP, I, p. 185.

82. James' Preface to Ferrari's Italian Edition of PP (1900) in PP, III, p. 1483.

83. Iser, p. 96.

84. Perry, II, 696.

85. The notable exception, of course, is Nietzsche. See Nehamas, pp. 13-41.

86. Goodman, *Ways*, pp. 6-7.

87. *Ibid.*, pp. 7-17.

88. See pp. 47-48.

89. Perry, II, p. 668.

90. Morse Peckham states that art is characterized by disorder, that is by "perceptual and semantic discontinuity . . . [which] is the source not only for error but also for culturally validated error, which we call, when it is validated, creativity." "Discontinuity in Art," *Poetics* 7 (1978), p. 229. See also *Man's Rage for Chaos* (Philadelphia: Chilton Books, 1965).

91. Quoted in Lloyd Morris, *William James: The Message of a Modern Mind* (New York: Greenwood, 1950), p. 14.

92. LWJ, I, p. 295.

93. Richard Rorty, *The Consequences of Pragmatism* (Minneapolis: University of Minnesota Press, 1982), p. xxxix.

94. Goodman, *Languages*, p. 33; see chapter 1, pp. 3-43.

Chapter 5

1. Lament: VRE, p. 117 ("Failure, then, failure! so the world stamps us at every turn. . . ."); lyric: p. 216 ("The flood we are borne on rolls [obstructions] so lightly under that their very contact is unfelt. . . ."), pp. 221-22 ("In youth and health, in summer, in the woods or on the mountains, there come days when the weather seems all whispering with peace. . . ."); satire: pp. 277-78, pp. 280-83 (". . . the intellect, as in this Louis, is originally no larger than a pin's head, and cherishes ideas of God of corresponding smallness."; hymn: p. 307; praise: pp. 285, 293-94 (saints "are the great torch-bearers of this belief, the tip of the wedge, the cleavers of the darkness. Like the single drops which sparkle in the sun as they are flung far ahead of the advancing edge of a wave-crest or of a flood, they show the way and are forerunners. . . ."); dark sayings: p. 308 ("This is a dark saying, I know. . . . Those who have ears to hear, let them hear. . . .").

2. *Ibid.*, pp. 211-12.

3. *Ibid.*, pp. 214-15.

4. *Ibid.*, p. 11.

5. There are important issues concerning the identification of the voice in a book with the person who wrote it, though I am not able to address them in this book. See Michel Foucault, "What Is an Author?" in *Language, Counter-Memory, Practice*, ed. Donald F. Bouchard (Ithaca: Cornell University Press, 1977); and Michael Riffaterre, *Text Production*, transl. Terese Lyons (New York: Columbia University Press, 1983), chapter 1. James himself would have no difficulty with the idea that an author's works represent multiple selves, though completely dissociating the author from his or her works would be anathema to him.

6. In the famous French correspondent passage, where he recounts his own vision of the "black-haired youth with greenish skin, entirely idiotic," and his realization, *"that shape am I."* VRE, pp. 134-35.

7. *Ibid.*, p. 80.

8. *Ibid.*, p. 289.

9. *Ibid.*, p. 394.

10. *Ibid.*, p. 79.

11. *Ibid.*, p. 119.

12. *Ibid.*, p. 240.

13. See also *Ibid.*, pp. 255-57, 289-91. James advocates a similar attitude in "The Moral Equivalent of War" (ERM, pp. 162-73) and in "Is Life Worth Living?" (WB, pp. 45-48).

14. In addition, James argues that the basis of value is "immediate luminousness, . . . philosophical reasonableness, and moral helpfulness." VRE, pp. 21-23.

15. *Ibid.*, p. 28.

16. *Ibid.*, p. 17.

17. James repeats this theme in his discussion of definitions in chapter 2 and of intuition and rationalism in chapter 3. See *Ibid.*, pp. 30-34, 66-67.

18. By the way, this is yet another example of the operation of the chaotic in James. Classifications are too rigid and distorting, and they are challenged by the fluidity of the living voice. Characteristically for the *Varieties*, the relationship between the rigid orders of classification and the fluidity of the living voice is disruptive: the voices do not challenge harmoniously as domesticated chaos would; they disrupt.

19. *Ibid.*, pp. 40, 44

20. *Ibid.*, p. 16.

21. It is important to note that the voices in this book do not speak of matters that are absolutely foreign to a reader. As James claims, they are not different in kind from other religious experiences, and the proof of that is our response to the passages in our reading. We do not read them as science fiction or as gothic; we respond to the suffering or exhilaration involved in them.

22. *Ibid.*, p. 14.

23. *Ibid.*, p. 56.

24. *Ibid.*, p. 61.

25. *Ibid.*, p. 91.

26. *Ibid.*, pp. 117, 123, 125.

27. *Ibid.*, pp. 157-58, 166-67, 178-79.

28. *Ibid.*, p. 191.

29. As Richard R. Niebuhr notes, the "teeming variety" of the book "together with the fervor and intensity that many of the testimonies exhibit" both enthrall and overwhelm the reader. "William James' Metaphysics of Religious Experience," in *Streams of Grace, The Second Neesima Lectures* (Kyoto, Japan: Doshisha University Press, 1983), p. 79.

30. VRE, p. 46.

Chapter 6

1. LWJ, II, p. 122.

2. For example in *Pragmatism*, "You see that pragmatism can be called religious, if you allow that religion can be pluralis-

tic or merely melioristic in type" (p. 144).

3. It is a pervasive theme in Foucault, but is particularly evident in "Two Lectures," *Power/Knowledge: Selected Interviews and Other Writings 1972-77,* ed. Colin Gordon, transl. Colin Gordon, Leo Marshall, John Mepham, and Kate Soper (New York: Pantheon, 1980).

4. This is, I admit, a bold statement, but I am not arguing that disorientation is a meaningless term. Indeed, as I later say, the chaotic depends upon disorientation. But it seems to me that except for very extreme cases—very early infancy and very extreme psychosis—humans achieve some sort of orientation. That is not to say that all orientations are equal: some function very poorly. But, as I argue, a literal disorientation does not seem to be possible, so rather than contrast orientation with disorientation, it makes better sense to evaluate various orientations on the basis of how well they function.

5. We might say that a genuine disorientation exists in the severely mentally ill, in very young infants, and perhaps in extreme cases of senility. In all cases there is not just a "mistaken" orientation or a harmful one, but an *absence* of it. But if I believe that I am Aurangzeb and seek temples to destroy, I am oriented, but not in a way that has any cultural sanction or much personal usefulness. To be literally disoriented, I must have no identity, and no sense of surroundings. As soon as I make discriminations between self and other and between meaningful and meaningless elements in my environment, I am oriented.

6. Gordon D. Kaufman, *The Theological Imagination: Constructing the Concept of God* (Philadelphia: Westminster Press, 1981), p. 32. For Kaufman, the symbol of God orients us more effectively than others because it is both humanizing and relativizing. See chapter 1, "Constructing the Concept of God," in *Theological Imagination,* pp. 21-57.

7. For Mircea Eliade, who also views the central religious function as orientation, the sacred founds the *world*. A hierophany "allows the world to be constituted, because it reveals the fixed point, the central axis for all future orientation." Eliade, *The Sacred and the Profane* (New York: Harcourt, 1959), p. 21. It is useful to compare Eliade with Kaufman because he sees the sacred orienting in many of the same ways Kaufman does. In addition he illumines

James because, for Eliade, ideas of chaos play an essential role in orientation, as do symbols, notions that I will address shortly.

8. In "On Orientation in Thinking," Kant uses the metaphor of finding our way in a dark room. Just as we can orient ourselves in the room if we grasp one known object, so we can find our way to our "true destination" by the use of postulates. The essay is in *Kant*, ed. Gabriele Rabel (Oxford: Clarendon Press, 1963), pp. 168-70. Kaufman traces his thinking about orientation back to this article and to Erich Fromm who states, "I understand by religion any system of thought and action shared by a group which gives the individual a frame of orientation and an object of devotion." Fromm, *Psychoanalysis and Religion* (New Haven: Yale University Press, 1950), p. 21. See especially chapter 3, pp. 21-64. Kaufman, personal communication.

9. Stephen Pepper calls such images "root metaphors." See Pepper, *World Hypotheses: A Study in Evidence* (Berkeley: University of California Press, 1942), pp. 91ff.

10. Kaufman, p. 35.

11. For Eliade, that which is outside of the world in which we are oriented is chaos. "Everything outside . . . is no longer a cosmos but a sort of 'other world,' a foreign, chaotic space, peopled by ghosts, demons, 'foreigners'." Chaos, then, is where there is no orientation; chaos and disorientation are synonymous. Eliade, p. 29.

12. Kaufman, pp. 39-41.

13. In spite of what Eliade says, *contrasting* chaos with orientation ("human beings cannot live in chaos"), it is nonetheless true that chaos orients for Eliade. First, simply as that which is to be avoided, that which lies "outside" and *must* be transformed into cosmos, chaos orients. It functions according to the definition I offered in chapter 2: Eliade's chaos contrasts with and challenges something that is more ordered, structured, or formed, namely cosmos. Neither Eliade himself nor the people he describes would be fully oriented without this image of the threatening chaos. In addition, Eliade speaks of chaos in another sense. Festivals that repeat the cosmogony involve a return to primordial chaos that acts to regenerate and purify. More generally, Eliade argues that water symbolizes "the universal sum of virtualities . . . the reservoir of all the possibilities of existence." And "immersion in water signifies regression to the preformal, reincorporation into the undifferentiated

mode of pre-existence," which is "at once purifying and regenerating." Hence, chaos not only orients by being placed "outside" orientation, it also functions from within. Eliade, pp. 34, 130-31.

14. See Friedrich Nietzsche, *Beyond Good and Evil*, transl. Walter Kaufman (New York: Vintage, 1966), p. 68; *Pragmatism*, p. 131; Kant, p. 169.

15. Let me note, again, that some orientations work better than others. So those whose orientation is inadequate are, in ordinary language, disoriented. By the way, Eliade seems to agree that there is no utter lack of orientation. He argues that a purely profane existence—that is, one completely lacking some notion of the sacred that orients—is never found. "To whatever degree he may have desacralized the world, the man who has made his choice in favor of the profane life never succeeds in completely doing away with religious behavior." Eliade, p. 23.

16. Viewed from a social, psychological, or medical perspective, these orientations may not be particularly adequate. The psychotic's rage prevents successful social interaction and may well be physically harmful to him or herself. Those are certainly criteria of adequate orientation. The infant's comfort works well for the time, but it is not an orientation that can continue for long. Nonetheless, both infant and psychotic are "placed" and "front" life. Neither utterly lacks orientation.

17. In this chapter I will use a different terminology for the two sorts of chaos since I am speaking here more generally than I have in the previous chapters. The terms that seem most useful to me are *hard* and *soft* chaos. The adjectives are purposively vague to gather much in, but I believe they communicate what I mean sufficiently well. The disruptive chaos that I have described in James is a species of "hard" chaos, and domesticated chaos is a subset of the "soft."

18. Pascal, section 72, p. 17.

19. For example, in *Fear and Trembling* (Princeton: Princeton University Press, 1968).

20. Karl Barth, *The Epistle to the Romans*, transl. Edwyn C. Hoskyns (London: Oxford University Press, 1968), pp. 110, 65.

21. Certainly the difference between James's sick souls and the healthy-minded is the value of disorientation.

22. For example, Robert Jay Lifton's discussion of nuclear weapons in *Indefensible Weapons* depends on disorientation. "The truth is that we have found no language, and perhaps there is none, to express the destructiveness, evil, and absurdity of the nuclear devices." We simply cannot even *imagine* it, he claims. And it is our attempt to use language, to make these weapons conventional, that is so dangerous. Yet, of course, we *can* imagine these weapons through such language as "absurdity" and "irrationality." Far from having *no* language, Lifton has some very powerful terms, but it is a discussion that insists on the orientation that is performed by utter disorientation. Lifton and Richard Falk, *Indefensible Weapons: The Political and Psychological Case Against Nuclearism* (New York: Basic, 1982), p. 108.

23. It is certainly true that meaninglessness is a similar symbol: we cannot have no meaning. Nothingness operates in the same fashion. Chaos in its "hard" sense does nothing that these others do not. It is different in its scope, being a term that at base refers to the entire cosmos, and, hence, it is particularly viable as a worldview. It also has mythological roots that enable us to orient ourselves with especial breadth and depth.

24. Mark Taylor, *Erring: A Postmodern A/theology* (Chicago: University of Chicago Press, 1984), p. 3.

25. Matthew Arnold, "Stanzas from the Grande Chartreuse."

26. Taylor, pp. 13, 13, 10.

27. Victor Turner, *The Ritual Process: Structure and Anti-Structure* (Chicago: Aldine, 1969), p. 95.

28. The cosmogonic chaos that Eliade writes of, the primordial "reservoir of possibilities" to which people return during festivals and that regenerates and purifies, is liminal and disorienting in a "soft" way.

29. Taylor, p. 15.

30. N.J. Girardot, "Chaos," *Encyclopedia of Religion*, III, ed. Mircea Eliade, (New York: Macmillan, 1987), pp. 213-18 . This work was published too late to be of any assistance in the development of my own thought about chaos, but it does seem that we agree about two kinds of chaos, though Girardot's sources are generally myths and mine are literary, philosophical, and theological. Another difference is that Girardot divided chaos into negative and

positive varieties while I have found it more useful to differentiate the constructive from the disruptive. Girardot's book on the theme of chaos in early Taoism is extremely stimulating, particularly on the value of chaos. Girardot, *Myth and Meaning in Early Taoism: The Theme of Chaos (hun-tun)* (Berkeley: University of California Press, 1983).

31. See Taylor, part 2, pp. 97-182.

32. *The Tragedy of King Lear*, act III, sc. ii, lines 1-9.

33. *Talks*, p. 152.

34. William Blake, "There Is No Natural Religion, All Religions Are One," *William Blake: The Complete Poems*, ed. Alicia Ostriker (London: Penguin, 1977), pp. 75-77.

35. Blake, "The Marriage of Heaven and Hell," p. 194.

36. Clifford Geertz, "Religion as a Cultural System," in *The Interpretation of Cultures* (New York: Basic, 1973), p. 90.

37. *Ibid.*

38. Paul Tillich, *The Dynamics of Faith* (New York: Harper, 1957), pp. 41-43; Ernst Cassirer, *Language and Myth* (New York: Dover, 1946), p. 8.

39. Eliade, p. 21.

40. T. S. Eliot, *Notes Towards the Definition of Culture* (New York: Harcourt, 1949), p. 30. Emphasis is Eliot's.

41. Samuel Taylor Coleridge, *Confessions of an Inquiring Spirit* (Stanford, Calif.: Stanford University Press, 1957), pp. 51-52.

42. Walter H. Beale, *A Pragmatic Theory of Rhetoric* (Carbondale: Southern Illinois University Press, 1987), pp. 104-5.

43. Kenneth Burke, *The Rhetoric of Religion* (Boston: Beacon, 1961), p. v.

Select Bibliography

Abernethy, Peter L. "Entropy in Pynchon's *The Crying of Lot 49.*" *Critique* 14, 2 (1972).

Adams, Henry. *The Education of Henry Adams*. Boston: Houghton Mifflin Company, 1918.

Allen, Gay Wilson. *William James: A Biography*. New York: The Viking Press, 1967.

Anderson, James William. *"William James' Depressive Period (1867-1872) and the Origins of His Creativity."* Ph.D., diss., University of Chicago, 1980.

Arnold, Matthew. "Stanzas from the Grande Chartreuse."

Bakhtin, Mikhail. *The Dialogic Imagination*. Ed. Michael Holquist. Transl. Caryl Emerson and Michael Holquist. Austin: University of Texas Press, 1981.

Barth, Karl. *The Epistle to the Romans*. Transl. Edwyn C. Hoskyns. London: Oxford University Press, 1968.

Barthes, Roland. "Introduction to the Structural Analysis of Narratives," in *Image—Music—Text*. Transl. Stephen Heath. New York: Hill and Wang, 1977.

Barzun, Jacques. *A Stroll with William James*. New York: Harper & Row Publishers, 1983.

Beale, Walter H. *A Pragmatic Theory of Rhetoric*. Carbondale: Southern Illinois University Press, 1987.

Blake, William. *William Blake: The Complete Poems*. Ed. Alicia Ostriker. London: Penguin, 1977.

Booth, Wayne C. Introduction to Mikhail Bakhtin, *Problems of Dostoevsky's Poetics*. Ed. and transl. Caryl Emerson. Minneapolis: University of Minnesota Press, 1984.

Brennan, Barnard P. *William James*. New York: Twayne, 1968.

Bruner, Jerome. *Actual Minds Possible Worlds*. Cambridge: Harvard University Press, 1986.

Buell, Lawrence. *Literary Transcendentalism: Style and Vision in the American Renaissance*. Ithaca: Cornell University Press, 1973.

Burgt, Robert J. *The Religious Philosophy of William James*. Chicago: Nelson-Hall, 1981.

Burke, Kenneth. *The Rhetoric of Religion*. Boston: Beacon Press, 1961.

Burnelli, Vincent. *Josiah Royce*. New York: Twayne, 1964.

Bush, Douglas. *Matthew Arnold: A Survey of His Poetry and Prose*. New York: Macmillan Publishing Co., 1971.

Cassirer, Ernst. *Language and Myth*. Transl. Suzanne K. Langer. New York: Dover, 1946.

Chopin, Kate. *The Awakening*. New York: Garrett Press, 1970.

Coleridge, Samuel Taylor. "On Poesy or Art," in *Biographia Literaria*. Ed. J. Shawcross. London: Oxford University Press, 1907.

————. *Biographia Literaria*. Eds. James Engell and W. Jackson Bate. *The Collected Works of Samuel Taylor Coleridge*. Princeton: Princeton University Press, 1983.

————. *Confessions of an Inquiring Spirit*. Stanford, Calif.: Stanford University Press, 1957.

Crites, Stephen. "The Narrative Quality of Experience." *Journal of the American Academy of Religion* 39, 3 (1971).

————. "Angels We Have Heard," in *Religion as Story*. Ed. James B. Wiggins. New York: Harper & Row Publishers, 1975.

Dean, William. "Radical Empiricism and Religious Art." *Journal of Religion* 61, 2 (April 1981).

Derrida, Jacques. *Of Gramatology*. Transl. Gayatri Chakrovorty Spivak. Baltimore: Johns Hopkins University Press, 1976.

Driver, Tom D. "Beckett by the Madeleine." *Columbia University Forum* 4, 3 (Summer 1961).

Edel, Leon. *Henry James: The Untried Years*. Philadelphia: J. B. Lippincot Company, 1953.

Eliade, Mircea. *The Sacred and the Profane*. New York: Harcourt, Brace, and World, 1959.

Eliot, T. S. *Notes Towards the Definition of Culture*. New York: Harcourt, Brace, 1949.

Estess, Ted. "The Inenarrable Contraption: Reflections on the Metaphor of Story." *Journal of the American Academy of Religions* 42, 3 (1974).

Federman, Raymond. *Journey to Chaos: Samuel Beckett's Early Fiction.* Berkeley: University of California Press, 1965.

Feinstein, Howard M. *Becoming William James.* Ithaca: Cornell University Press, 1984.

Foucault, Michel. "Two Lectures," in *Power/Knowledge: Selected Interviews and Other Writings 1972-77.* Ed. Colin Gordon. Transl. Colin Gordon, Leo Marshall, John Mepham, and Kate Soper. New York: Pantheon Books, 1980.

Fowler, Alastair. *Kinds of Literature: An Introduction to the Theory of Genres and Modes.* Cambridge: Harvard University Press, 1982.

Frankenberry, Nancy. *Religion and Radical Empiricism.* Albany: State University of New York Press, 1987.

Freud, Sigmund. *An Autobiographical Study.* Transl. James Strachey. London: Hogarth Press, 1935.

————. *New Introductory Lectures on Psychoanalysis* transl. W. J. H. Sprout. New York: W. W. Norton & Company, 1933.

Fromm, Erich. *Psychoanalysis and Religion.* New Haven: Yale University Press, 1950.

Geertz, Clifford. "Religion as a Cultural System," in *The Interpretation of Cultures.* New York: Basic Books, 1973.

Genette, Gerard. *Figures of Literary Discourse.* New York: Columbia University Press, 1982.

————. *Narrative Discourse: An Essay in Method.* Transl. Jane E. Lewin. Ithaca: Cornell University Press, 1980.

Girardot, N. J. "Chaos," in *Encyclopedia of Religion.* Ed. Mircea Eliade. New York: Macmillan Publishing Co., 1987.

————. *Myth and Meaning in Early Taoism: The Theme of Chaos (huntun)* Berkeley: University of California Press, 1983.

Gleick, James. *Chaos: Making a New Science.* New York: The Viking Press, 1987.

von Goethe, Johann Wolfgang. *Faust.* Transl. Louis MacNeice. New York: Oxford University Press, 1951.

Goodman, Nelson. *Languages of Art.* Indianapolis, Indiana: Hackett Publishing, 1976.

176   THE CREATION OF CHAOS

———. *Of Minds and Other Matters*. Cambridge: Harvard University Press, 1984.

———. *Ways of Worldmaking*. Indianapolis: Hackett, 1978.

Halle, Louis J. *Out of Chaos*. Boston: Houghton Mifflin Company, 1977.

Hampshire, Stuart. "Amiable Genius." Review of *William James: Writings 1902-1910*. Ed. Bruce Kuklick. *New York Review of Books*, 35, 2 (1988), pp. 17-20.

Hesla, David H. *The Shape of Chaos: An Interpretation of the Art of Samuel Beckett*. Minneapolis: University of Minnesota Press, 1971.

Hobbes, Thomas. *Leviathan: or the Matter. Form and Power of a Commonwealth, Ecclesiasticall or Civill*. Ed. A. R. Weller. Cambridge: Cambridge University Press, 1935.

Holquist, Michael. Introduction to Mikhail Bakhtin, *Dialogic Imagination*. Ed. Michael Holquist. Transl. Caryl Emerson and Michael Holquist. Austin: University of Texas Press, 1981.

Hughes, Merritt Y. Introduction to *Paradise Lost*, in *John Milton: Complete Poems and Major Prose*. Ed. Hughes. New York: Odyssey Press, 1957.

Iser, Wolfgang. *The Act of Reading: A Theory of Aesthetic Response*. Baltimore: Johns Hopkins Press, 1978.

James, Alice. *The Diary of Alice James*. Ed. Leon Edel. New York: Penguin, 1982.

James, Henry. Preface to the New York Edition, *Portrait of a Lady*. Ed. Robert D. Bamberg. New York: W. W. Norton & Company, 1975.

———. *A Small Boy and Others*. New York: Charles Scribner's Sons, 1913.

Jones, Ernest. *The Life and Work of Sigmund Freud*. 2 vols. New York: Basic Books, 1953-57.

Kant, Immanuel. *Critique of Judgment*. Transl. J. H. Bernard. New York: Hafner Press, 1951.

———. "On Orientation in Thinking," in *Kant*. Ed. Gabriele Rabel. Oxford: Clarendon Press, 1963.

Kaufman, Gordon D. *An Essay on Theological Method*. Rev. ed. Missoula, Mont.: Scholar's Press, 1979.

———. *The Theological Imagination: Constructing the Concept of God*.

Philadelphia: Westminster Press, 1981.

Kierkegaard, Soren. *Fear and Trembling*. Transl. Walter Lowrie. Princeton: Princeton University Press, 1968.

LaGuardia, David M. *Advance on Chaos: The Sanctifying Imagination of Wallace Stevens*. Hanover, N.H.: University Press of New England, 1983.

Lewalski, Barbara K. *Paradise Lost and The Rhetoric of Literary Forms*. Princeton: Princeton University Press, 1985.

Levinson, Henry Samuel. *The Religious Investigations of William James*. Chapel Hill: University of North Carolina Press, 1981.

Lifton, Robert J. and Falk, Richard. *Indefensible Weapons: The Political and Psychological Case Against Nuclearism*. New York: Basic Books, 1982.

Mackey, Louis. *Kierkegaard: A Kind of Poet*. Philadelphia: University of Pennsylvania Press, 1971.

Martland, Thomas R. *The Metaphysics of William James and John Dewey: Process and Structure in Philosophy and Religion*. New York: Philosophical Library, 1963.

Martz, Louis L. *The Poetry of Meditation: A Study of English Religious Literature of the Seventeenth Century*. New Haven: Yale University Press, 1954.

Milton, John. *John Milton: Complete Poems and Major Prose*. Ed. Merritt Y. Hughes. New York: Odyssey Press, 1957.

Morris, Lloyd. *William James: The Message of a Modern Mind*. New York: Greenwood, 1950.

Myers, Gerald E. *William James: His Life and Thought*. New Haven: Yale University Press, 1986.

Nash, Roderick. *Wilderness and the American Mind*. New Haven: Yale University Press, 1967.

Nehamas, Alexander. *Nietzsche: Life as Literature*. Cambridge: Harvard University Press, 1985.

Niebuhr, H. Richard. *Radical Monotheism and Western Culture*. New York: Harper & Row, Publishers, 1943.

Niebuhr, Richard R. "William James' Metaphysics of Religious Experience," in *Streams of Grace: Studies of Jonathan Edwards, Samuel Taylor Coleridge, and William James*. The Neesima Lectures. Kyoto, Japan:

Doshisha University Press, 1983.

Nietzsche, Friedrich. *Beyond Good and Evil.* Transl. Walter Kaufman. New York: Vintage, 1966.

Novalis, *Schriften.* 3 Leipzig: Bibliographisches Institut U.G., n.d.

Ovid. *Metamorphoses.* Transl. Rolfe Humphries. Bloomington: Indiana University Press, 1957.

———. *Ovid's Metamorphoses in Fifteen Books.* Translated by the most Eminent Hands. London: Jacob Tonsun, 1717.

Pascal, Blaise. *Pensees.* New York: E. P. Dutton & Co., 1958.

Peckham, Morse. "Discontinuity in Art." *Poetics* 7 (1978).

———. *Man's Rage for Chaos.* Philadelphia: Chilton Books, 1965.

Pepper, Stephen C. *World Hypotheses: A Study in Evidence.* Berkeley: University of California Press, 1942.

Proudfoot, Wayne. *Religious Experience.* Berkeley: University of California Press, 1985.

Riffaterre, Michael. *Text Production.* Transl. Terese Lyons. New York: Columbia University Press, 1983.

Rorty, Richard. "Pragmatism, Relativism, and Irrationalism," in *The Consequences of Pragmatism.* Minneapolis: University of Minnesota Press, 1982.

Royce, Josiah. *The Problem of Christianity.* 2 vols. New York: Macmillan Publishing Co., 1914.

———. *William James and Other Essays on the Philosophy of Life.* New York: Macmillan Publishing Co., 1911.

Ruddick, Lisa. "Fluid Symbols in American Modernism: William James, Gertrude Stein, George Santayana, and Wallace Stevens," in *Allegory, Myth, and Symbol.* Harvard English Studies. Ed. Morton W. Bloomfield. Cambridge: Harvard University Press, 1981.

de Sales, Frances. *Treatise on the Love of God.* 1616.

Seigfried, Charlene Haddock. *Chaos and Context: A Study in William James.* Athens: Ohio University Press, 1978.

———. "Vagueness and the Adequacy of Concepts: In Defense of Wm. James's Picturesque Style," *Philosophy Today* 26 (Winter) 1982.

Shakespeare. *The Tragedy of King Lear,* in *Shakespeare: The Complete*

Works. Ed. G. B. Harrison. New York: Harcourt, Brace and World, 1968.

————. *The Tragedy of Othello*, in *Complete Works*.

————. *The Tragedy of Troilus and Cressida*, in *Complete Works*.

Smart, Ninian. *Worldviews: Crosscultural Explorations of Human Beliefs*. New York: Charles Scribner's Sons, 1983.

Stevens, Wallace. *Collected Poems*. New York: Alfred A. Knopf, 1976.

Taylor, Mark. *Erring: A Postmodern A/theology*. Chicago: University of Chicago Press, 1984.

Thorslev, Peter L., Jr. *Romantic Contraries: Freedom and Destiny*. New Haven: Yale University Press, 1984.

Tillich, Paul. *The Dynamics of Faith*. New York: Harper & Row, Publishers, 1957.

————. *Systematic Theology*. 3 vols. Chicago: University of Chicago Press, 1951.

Todorov, Tzvetan. *The Poetics of Prose*. Transl. Richard Howard. Ithaca: Cornell University Press, 1977.

Turner, Victor. *The Ritual Process: Structure and Anti-Structure*. Chicago: Aldine Publishing Company, 1969.

Voltaire. "Well, Everything Is Well," in *Candide or Optimism*. Transl. Robert M. Adams. New York: W. W. Norton & Company, 1966.

Index